# Piece of Cake

## MY WILD RIDE FROM BANKING TO BAKING

*Sweet reading!*
*Melissa Bunnen Jernigan*

### MELISSA BUNNEN JERNIGAN
#### *with* LISA CERASOLI

STORY MERCHANT BOOKS
LOS ANGELES • 2021

Piece of Cake

ISBN-13: 978-1-970157-24-6

Story Merchant Books
400 S. Burnside Avenue #11B
Los Angeles, CA 90036
www.storymerchantbooks.com

www.529bookdesign.com
Interior design: Lauren Michelle
Cover: Claire Moore

www.pieceofcakeinc.com

Instagram: @pieceofcake

For James, Jack, Lindy, all my family and friends, and my Piece of Cake family who've endured this journey with me, and for everyone who buys Piece of Cake cakes and asks me how this whole thing went down: this book is for you.

# Piece of Cake

## MY WILD RIDE FROM BANKING TO BAKING

MELISSA BUNNEN JERNIGAN
*with* LISA CERASOLI

## *What is this book, anyway?*

It's a memoir, a business book, a book about baked goods that's not about baking. It's a comedy, a comedy of errors, a story about family and friendship.

This book is about a journey. A hero's journey? If we're all heroes, then, sure. This is a book about my heroes. It's about listening to your mother, to the voices in your head (just some of them!), and to the universe. It's a book about madness and mayhem, hard work and happiness, surrender and synergy.

This is a book about doing it my way. Thanks for being a part of it but stay tuned.

Because this is just the end of the beginning....

Piece of Cake

# INTRODUCTION

For whatever reason, people like to hear how we started Piece of Cake. Maybe it's because the company was founded by two women who'd abandoned Corporate America to do something less traditional. Maybe it's because the company's success belies its modest beginnings in a one-hundred-square-foot condo kitchen. Maybe the tale has appeal because baking cakes is a tangible sort of undertaking unlike nanotechnology. Maybe Piece of Cake's story is intriguing because anybody can bake a cake because, surely, everyone has.

*Or have they?*

## —Fall 1985—

No sooner had the latest update on our infant company—started two months back—escaped my lips than my mother, Lucinda, sped into the living room, where my dad was half-listening to Tom Brokaw, half-reading the *Atlanta Journal*. "Bobby! Bobby, Melissa doubled her business. She doubled it! I told you they could do it."

"She'd better watch out before somebody finds out she doesn't know how to bake a cake." Dad chuckled.

"She reads one article in the *Wall Street Journal* and turns into Betty Crocker overnight? *Who does that?*" my brother, Robb, asked. "Who's buying these cakes, anyway? Belinda? How do people even know they exist? She gives new meaning to the term soft sell."

"Your sister, Belinda, is busy with the baby," Mom reminded him.

"Does that business partner of hers know how to bake a cake?" Dad asked to no one in particular. Then, to my brother, he said, "I've never seen your sister boil an egg or even crack one now that I think about it. These are the real questions here."

Robb the lawyer had inherited Dad the doctor's cynicism toward all things impractical, and baking cakes as a way of life fell under the umbrella of impractical. It made sense that they were united in their "awe" of my new career endeavor.

But Mom hurdled their ridicule like she was Edwin Moses at the Olympics. She was my biggest fan (as I was hers). Both Robb and Belinda, my older siblings, have always said the umbilical cord was never severed. But Mom wasn't exaggerating this time—I *had* doubled the business overnight.

Needing the real dirt, Robb popped his head into the kitchen. "What's 'double'?"

"Four," I said.

"*Hundred?*" he asked.

I shook my head.

"Four...*tee?*" He was heading in the right direction.

"Four. I got two orders on Wednesday and on Thursday, well...."

Knowing he couldn't begrudge those sales, he cracked a smile, and then we both worked hard not to laugh out loud, as we didn't want to ruin Mom's celebration.

But Dad was right. I could barely boil an egg, and I had started a cake baking and delivery business with my friend,

Helen Cleveland, without either one of us having ever baked a single cake.

○ ○ ○

Even though we'd jumped cannonball-style into the deep pool of hopeful entrepreneurs without life jackets or even a two-*woman* raft on standby, we weren't the only people searching for our bliss in the late eighties. Don't forget this was before the internet, before you could order dog food or flip-flops or mattresses at a place called "online" and have them delivered to your door. This was before hybrid cars and drive-through coffee bars, before corporations like Starbucks became a household name—if you can imagine such an archaic time. The Seattle-based coffeehouse had served its first latte just one year prior. Imagine this time in America if you can.

I had always had big dreams—Starbucks big (and I still do). I just wasn't talking about them. They were keeping me up at night, though. The voices have never stopped chattering in my head.

About this time, halfway around the world, another visionary, Susumu Kakinuma (also a twenty-something with an entrepreneurial spirit on par with ours) wanted to bring his career aspirations to life. Since he'd been a teen, he hadn't been able to get the opening scene from *Saturday Night Fever*—where John Travolta eats two slices of Lenny's pizza sandwich-style while strutting down the streets of Brooklyn—out of his mind. *Can you picture it, too, now?* He thought this type of cuisine could be relevant in his homeland of Tokyo, believing in his heart there was a need for it, just as Helen and I believed in the sweet, rich, magical power of cake delivered straight to your door.

So, to learn the art of pizza making, the voices in Susumu's head told him to go to Naples and find an apprenticeship. The generations-thick pizza makers of Italy balked at his outlandish request, turning him down repeatedly. He had to eat his way through the countryside and practice duplicating his findings. He did this for a year, then took that education back home, perfecting just two types of pizza, eventually opening Seirinkan, or what would become known as "the original pizza place in Tokyo." His pizza has become the standard by which all other pizzas in Japan are judged to this day.

Like the empirical Susumu Kakinuma, we wanted to be original, inspired, and successful.

While I waited for inspiration to strike, "the original Tokyo pizza guy" marched, singularly focused, appetite in tow, into every pizza parlor in Naples to master the art of pizza making.

I wasn't without direction, though. I was on alert, waiting to be inspired. Meanwhile, however, Helen and I were doing everything but becoming expert bakers.

When we opened for business, we didn't know squat about our product. Not only had neither of us ever baked a cake, I had neither watched my mother bake one nor ever made a "practice" one in my Easy-Bake Oven (a much-wanted Christmas gift in '67 that became more of a bookshelf than anything). My pocket-sized condo—the location where

Piece of Cake was birthed—didn't even house a cakepan when our first order came in.

Never mind an egg, Helen and I hadn't cracked a cookbook or studied the art of baking by shadowing a pastry chef. And, we didn't eat our way through every bakery in America for a year to learn how—although, back then, my sweet tooth would've loved that. Those things just didn't occur to us. Personally, I've always done things differently, believing there's more than one way to crack an egg.

Born from a desire to create something unique, something of value, and to have fun while doing it, Piece of Cake has been going strong for over thirty-five years. We employ over 125 "Cakers" sprinkled throughout ten stores in Atlanta, including one at Hartsfield-Jackson Atlanta International, the busiest airport in the world.

## WE TAKE THE CAKE. *ANYWHERE.*

We sell around a million baked goods annually—and we have a celebrity following, delivering to stars whose names I'm too shy to list. (You'll have to trust me on this or google it!)

We kept it simple in the beginning just like Susumu did, offering only three types of cakes. But that's where our similarities end, because we cracked the eggs our own way and I'll be damned if it didn't work.

This is the story of starting a company on pocket change, of working twenty-hour days with no days off in sight, of losing my home to sacks of sugar and flour and ovens galore. This is a story about cakes cooling atop lampshades, about nervous breakdowns, wandering pot dealers, babies, puppies, Cakers, and bakers. This is a story about the *original* housewives of Atlanta and the homeless, too. (They were working for me!) It's a story about a car called The Bomb, and a place called Pamland that exists to be sure, but you won't find it on any GPS system to date.

Piece of Cake is a place where autonomy ruled and that was the only rule, where the employee handbook was a WWII romance novel blanketed in cake dust, where people turned when they needed directions, the latest gossip, or some armchair psychology. It's where former financial investors were caught with mops in their hands (you know who you are), exchanging three-piece suits and stress of investing for some good old-fashioned fun and a little slice of sanity. A lot of well-known Atlantans did time here. And now their kids are doing time here.

I was a liberal arts major. You won't find my business philosophy being taught at Harvard Business School, at onlineMBA.com, or any institution in between. But you will find it here.

*Piece of Cake: My Wild Ride from Banking to Baking* is a career manual for folks who know little about business, a cookbook for those who've never thought about baking, and a *what-are-you-waiting-for* guide to pursuing your dreams.

Seriously, what are you waiting for?

This is the story of doing it my way....

# PART I

## TWO COLLEGE GRADS, ONE OVEN RACK, ZERO BAKING SKILLS

"Fake it till you bake it."

—Helen Cleveland
Cofounder, Piece of Cake

# 1

## NOTHING'S BETTER THAN A CAKE BREAK

Before doing a reverse dive into the deep end of my future—
*"Melissa Bunnen, I hereby sentence you to 9-to-5 for life! A
degree in American Studies? Are you joking?"*—I got a degree
in (yes) American Studies from Hollins University in Virginia.
Hollins is one of the oldest institutions for higher learning for
women in the country. I loved school. It was at Hollins where
I had lots of fun, didn't study too hard, and made lifelong
friends. But then, four years later with degrees in hand, like
fish in a tank when you get too close, *bam*, my friends and I
scattered in all directions.

I moved back home to Atlanta, where, to celebrate
graduating, I took a quick trip out West with three girlfriends.
Four Chicks in a Chevy Van. It was a Hunter S.
Thompson/Jack Kerouac-style excursion (minus the sex,
drugs, and verse, of course). Two months after that, I began
working at First Atlanta Bank, which was the opposite of
traversing the West Coast in a Chevy van with your
girlfriends.

I had been a teller during my last summer in college. This was what had gotten me into the management trainee program. I enjoyed working, but the inflexible schedule didn't suit my lifestyle. I also felt like the subject matter, the glossary of terms I was to put to memory—APR, APY, HELOC, FDIC, NSF, SSL—were mind numbing. I honestly couldn't tell you how much I was retaining. Was this my destiny? I could see my life laid out in a series of acronyms from DOB to RIP and I wasn't happy about it.

## A BAD FIRST JOB CAN BE A GREAT BEGINNING

I had a great time with the people that worked at First Atlanta, though. And it seemed someone was always having a birthday, every single day. This made it tolerable for people like me who weren't all that interested in the nuts, bolts, and numbers that go into banking. I've often wondered if that was the point of all those celebrations. Did the higher-ups know the day-to-day grind, the sameness of it all, was stupefying and that regular breaks laced with sugar would help get some of us through the day, the year, a lifetime?

And so, with no vision of my future in sight, I moved from the credit department to mortgages to trusts.

And life went on.

—1984—

"That's twenty, forty, sixty, eighty—one. And twenty, forty, sixty, eighty—two." And, KMN.[1] Even though I wasn't tellering all day, that's what it felt like. Monotonous. When I die, if TPTB[2] decide to send me south for all of eternity, I know I'll be an accountant and every day will be April the fourteenth.

One day out of the blue, Kenan, a college friend from Richmond, Virginia, phoned and said, "You do not strike me as a banker." She thought I'd be a great fit to manage Pine Factory, a new furniture store opening at a nearby mall. I interviewed and signed on.

I was making a teensy bit more money, which Dad loved, as that was language he understood. But I mainly liked my new title: manager, which was acronym-free like everything else at the furniture store (language I understood). Plus, my sister, Belinda, was working across the hall at the dance center. Leggings galore! This was a satisfying change, and life became about 7.3 percent more interesting.

Still, I wasn't inspired. Belinda said she'd watch me spend my days crossing my legs one way, then re-crossing them the other way when the leg on the bottom went numb. I was the type of person who needed commotion, the kind that sitting on a bisque-colored, micro-suede sectional reading self-helps was not providing.

I enrolled in two marketing classes at Georgia State. For a whole semester, that created some balance—but mainly it got me thinking that many of my college friends had spent time in

---

[1] Kill Me Now
[2] The Powers That Be

NYC during summer breaks, just to get the city-life experience. I had never done that. As I didn't see rearranging furniture as my destiny, I phoned an aunt and uncle who lived on the Upper East Side and asked if I could stay with them.

In a jiffy (how I did most things), I found employment with Union Settlement in Harlem, a nonprofit that provided education, wellness, and community-building programs. They were celebrating their Centennial Anniversary and throwing an epic bash. I was hired as assistant to the board chair, a party planner, essentially.

It was a job and I was in New York City and that was the point.

## IF IT STOPS BEING FUN, GET OUT!

# 2

## A SLICE OF NYC

I didn't know anyone in New York City. My aunt and uncle weren't going to hit Times Square or go to the Lincoln Center or a jazz or comedy club with me. They were consumed with their own careers and philanthropic endeavors, and they traveled to DC frequently, too. My younger cousin, William, who was taking a gap year, lived there, too. So that was fun.

Regardless of being alone in the Big Apple, I felt lucky. NYC seemed like an extension of college, another opportunity to explore and focus on letting go, hoping inspiration would find me.

In this in-between place, a typical day meant I'd leave at the crack of dawn to take the subway to work and come home at sundown to a generally empty home. This scenario was not what I'd envisioned from the movies, but I went with it.

Yup, it'd be just me, the sound of silence, and the *Wall Street Journal*—my uncle's paper of choice—waiting in their postbox along with the rest of the mail, which was hardly ever for me. I'd never read that paper before, but for some reason I picked it up one afternoon.

An article about how, one day, the growing trend across America was going to be home-and-office delivery caught my eye. And not just in New York City and not just Chinese food, the article said the trend would spread across America. That sounded like more fun than crunching numbers and being married to a punch card. I was engrossed in the article when my uncle and William walked in.

I felt my cheeks warm, like a kid who'd been caught with her hand in the cookie jar, a teenager caught sneaking into an R-rated movie, a wannabe adult caught reading, well, the very adult *Wall Street Journal*.

As if sensing my unease, Uncle Frank said, "You know, Melissa, nonprofit is great, but you're smart enough to do something different and have whatever nonprofit you want on the side."

William gave me a shrug and a half-nod. Then, they loosened their ties and left to change for dinner.

Was it that obvious I was snooping for direction anywhere I could get it? I, the twenty-five-year-old party planner, was so off-course that I was searching for answers in the *Wall Street Journal?* Is that what I looked like to the outside world? Egads.

*Could I really write my own ticket?*

Maybe my uncle was just making conversation and said that because the gala I'd been planning was around the corner. I was hired for a temporary position, after all.

Still basically friendless, my thoughts and I would flee to Central Park every chance we got.

I'd watch people exercise, play with their kids, walk their dogs, fight and make up. It filled my soul. One time, I saw these young parents teaching their little boy how to ride his bike without the training wheels. Not into it, he screamed, "I knew you both hated me!" That has stuck with me to this day.

Anyway, on the heels of Union Settlement's Centennial Celebration came news that Belinda was pregnant with her first child and my Aunt Phoebe had been diagnosed with cancer. So, I did what I thought was right and practical and moved back home to be near family.

Slice of NYC. ✔

—August 1985—

It had been a few years since I'd graduated from college. And there I was, back in Atlanta, adrift in my pool of destiny. Again.

As I was getting ready to walk my lab, Moe, from the living room window of my condo, I spotted Helen parking her Honda.

She lived in a unit across the parking lot. We originally met when we both moved into this crappy but charming, old house in Buckhead with a mutual friend after college. Helen was forty-five minutes from the clothing retailers where she was employed, so she'd have to leave before me. To get to our shared bathroom, she'd have to traipse through my bedroom every morning to shower. The quickest way to get to know someone is this! Bonding on steroids was what we called it.

When we moved into the two vacant rooms in the Victorian-style house, Helen was dating Dave, a guy she'd met at the University of Georgia, who was a friend of Belinda's from high school. When they got married, they bought a condo. Coincidentally, I'd purchased one, too. Who knows who bought one first, but our doors were exactly 78 steps apart by Helen's count.

But it wasn't long after we moved into our new homes that I left for my NYC adventure. I came back with a job lined up doing marketing for one of Coca-Cola's vendors but, then, two days before I was supposed to start, the job fell through.

Helen had mentioned that she was up for being inspired, too, so by five o'clock daily, we'd usually be itching to socialize and brainstorm.

As she stepped out of the car, she cranked her neck, looking for a sign of life in my condo.

I cracked the window. "Helen!"

"You free tonight?"

"Yup!"

"Gimme fifteen to say hi to Dave and change."

"Yup!"

# 3

## THIS BUSINESS IS NUTS
## (OR, IS IT?)

My mother was never the traditional, stay-at-home-mom type. She was on a million boards, for starters. Normal boards at first—school, hospital—and then, she moved into committing herself to boards for the arts, the High Museum being the main one nowadays. (Yes, nowadays, and she's ninety! She'll be releasing another photography book shortly.)

Around 1970, we went on a family trip to Machu Picchu, Peru. Mom took a Super 8 camera, shooting and filming us like crazy. Honestly, it was more of a work vacation for everyone (Mom's orders). Then, she went home and signed up for an editing class, which was the only way to edit film and learn how to develop photos back then. She fell head over heels in love with photography after that.

A light went on.

At nineteen, mother had been invited to ski with the US Olympic team, but her father had become gravely ill and she couldn't leave him. She had many interests. She was an expert equestrian. But, her moment of inspiration/clarity/self-discovery happened when she held her first camera. I wanted something akin to that in my life.

Fifteen minutes and 78 steps later, Helen was at my place.

Different people connect for different reasons, and we both had an innate need to have purpose-driven careers. We got right to it.

"If we're going to do this, I just don't want to be a slave to alarm clocks and timecards for the next four decades. What if Dave and I want to have babies?" she said.

"Sure, of course. We want to be able to make babies, make our own hours, make money, make whatever we want."

"A laundry delivery service? We talked about that last week," she said.

We had two lists started. One had things we didn't want to do for the rest of our lives, like be a slave to the stringent structure if Corporate America. The other had business ideas. "Right, but, even though we want to be around people, do we really want to be around their dirty underwear?"

"That does feel awfully interactive, even for us," Helen agreed.

"We're *people* people not *people's dirty underwear* people."

"Right. Dog walking...? It's sort of a delivery service. Pet grooming at home?"

"We're not qualified. Or are we? Are you? Do you need a license for that?"

"You said it didn't matter whether we're qualified," Helen reminded me.

"To a degree. I mean, we're not gonna become race car drivers."

"Please promise me we're not going to become race car drivers." Helen was always a titch concerned about the lengths to which I'd go when I believed in something. Plus, I've always had a need for speed and really enjoy pinballing my way through traffic on the highway.

When I didn't swear to never bring that up again, she gave me a look.

"Yes, I promise. I don't even look good in a jumpsuit. That's nuts."

"It is nuts, like your other business idea: This Business Is Nuts."

"No, This Business Is Nuts is less nuts and maybe something we should still entertain," I suggested.

"Then we might as well put the shortbread idea back on the table."

"Except, my mother says that if the shortbread's on the table, I'll eat it all. She says history's proven this and it'd be a bad idea over time."

"Okay. No laundry, no dogs, no nuts, no shortbread," Helen confirmed. "You sure we want to deliver something?"

"That's what the article said, that home and office delivery will become big business, which sounds like a big deal," I said. "Hey, you want to grab a bite to eat? I'm starving."

"Sure, but I'm not very hungry. It was Bonnie's birthday. She's our retail manager, and I had this humongous piece of cake before leaving. God knows why. I wasn't even hungry.

11

Probably boredom. I'm always clock-watching by mid-afternoon."

"Oh, my god, when I was at the bank, that was the best. Cake. But there's no getting around it. Doesn't matter if you're not hungry or doing Weight Watchers, when someone passes you a piece of birthday cake, you take it. You can't say, "None for me, thanks, I'm pregnant," like with alcohol. It's plain rude not to accept a piece, like cutting-someone-off-in-traffic rude."

"Yeah, that's why I think I ate it. I didn't want to cut the birthday girl off in traffic when she handed it to me."

"Yeah," I said, moving past dinner and fantasizing about dessert. "What kind of cake? Was it marble? I love it when that happens. Sweet birthday surprise. Someone cuts the cake. You're hoping for white, maybe chocolate, maybe you're on the fence, and, *bam*, it's both!"

And that's when it hit us—*bam*—our *aha* moment.

"Cake," we both said.

"We could bake and deliver cakes!" I was getting excited, even at this fetal stage in the development of the company.

"And this could be our money maker? You think so, Melissa?"

"Everyone loves cake. I just made that argument."

"Okay, but should we research that?"

"You mean go to the library?" I asked. "Go door to door and take a survey?"

"We're not Avon Ladies."

"We are not." It was official, for me. This was going to be our moneymaker, our future.

My light went on.

Two years of banking finally made sense—it was so I could be around all that cake. And my stint in New York City had purpose in hindsight. It was about getting me alone in a room with a *Wall Street Journal* on the rare time I'd be in the mood to pick it up.

"*Your move, Melissa, I did all the legwork.*" The Universe was all up in my headspace.

It was true. The message from the *WSJ* had clung to my temporal lobe like dew on grass on any-morning Atlanta. Then, for almost a year, my destiny waited patiently until this very moment. Until my light went on.

Plus, this cake baking adventure sounded much safer than becoming the first female race car drivers, and it was better than death by shortbread. "We need to move on this."

"We *could* actually start by taking a survey," Helen suggested.

"Okay. Um, I have cake for all my birthdays. Do you?"

"Yup."

"And, Bonnie had cake, and, hold on." And out the door I dashed to the condo next door.

Forty-seven seconds later, I ran back in. "Ed in 212 eats cake on all his birthdays, and he had cake today at work for Tim or Tom's, too. We're five for five. You, me, Bonnie, Ed, and Tim or Tom."

"Five out of five people surveyed eat cake on their birthday."

"Cake it is," I confirmed.

And then we sat in silence for a bit, floating in the euphoria of having landed on a business idea that wowed us both. We wouldn't have to invest a ton of capital upfront or worry about a storage facility—we weren't manufacturing thousands of pet rocks—this was perfect.

Then, thirty seconds after that, Helen had to go and ask this question: "Have you ever baked a cake?"

"No. You?"

"Do cupcakes count?"

"Yes. No."

"Then, no."

I wasn't going to let that hiccup stop us. "Hey, Aunt Phoebe's housekeeper, Bertha, bakes one mean chocolate cake. It's got all these levels—"

"Layers."

"Layers. And this thick, chocolatey frosting. It's scrape-it-off-the-fork-with-your-teeth thick."

"Fudge frosting."

"*Yes.*"

"Okay, so, how do we get that recipe?" Helen asked.

"I think we ask my aunt to ask Bertha for it."

"Just like that?"

"Sure, piece of cake."

# 4

## GIRLS JUST WANT TO HAVE FUN
## (AND MAKE MONEY!)

"You're what? You're quitting your job to bake cakes?" Helen's dad asked. Although, it wasn't a question so much as an accusation. I know this for fact, as I could hear him through the phone.

"No, no, I'm not quitting my job. Not yet. I'll work on the new business in my off-hours. Melissa's going in full force until we get established."

"Baking cakes."

"Yes."

"Baking cakes. About which she knows nothing."

"Yes. She's never baked a cake."

"Can you hear it out loud, Helen?"

"I know it sounds crazy, but we've thought about it, we've had meetings, we even made lists. We made lists, Dad. This is what we're doing."

We understood why Helen's father was taken aback. This was out of character for her, too. She forged ahead, though. She had to. She was on the lip of the wave of hope, ready to catch the tube and sail into cake-baking celebrity with Yours Truly.

"Who came up with this cockamamie idea, anyway?" her dad demanded.

She shrugged, not that he could see her, but her silence said it all.

He finally asked, "What do you know about baking cakes?"

"I've made cupcakes."

"That doesn't count." At least we were united on that front.

"Then...nothing!" she snapped.

That's when he slammed the phone down and hung up.

Then Helen slammed the phone down. (This was back when you could do that.)

And that was that. After sleeping on our big business idea and having broken the news to both sets of parents, we were off!

I'd met her parents for the first time at her wedding. She was from New Jersey, so the opportunity hadn't come up sooner. Our dads could have been clones, both so dapperly dressed in their Brooks Brothers attire, except her dad was a businessman. Other than that, they even carried themselves in the same manner. They were educated, reserved, cordial, practical, hardworking family men who fell into step naturally with the ways of the world.

Helen had thrown him for a real loop.

My father, well, let's just say for a very short window, my dad could tell his friends that his son was a lawyer, one daughter was a teacher, and the other was in banking. That satisfied everyone. I'd shattered the vision he had for his children as adults with the proclamation, "I'm starting a cake baking and delivery company in my condo with Helen." He didn't know what to say about my new career path. It was literally incomprehensible to him.

When we did launch Piece of Cake, Dad would manage to stumble through his children's list of achievements, and, when he got to "my bit," it would end up ironically sounding like a pitch.

*"Yes, the kids are great. Robb's a lawyer, Belinda's a teacher, which is perfect for raising a family. And, Melissa, well, she's baking, um, very good cakes. But don't take my word for it. You should order some for your next event or meeting or what have you. They're very good cakes. Moist. Natural ingredients. Real butter. Top notch, these cakes...."*

Despite the inner horror of it all, he was our biggest, early supporter.

Two days later, Bertha handed over her triple-layer chocolate cake with the fudge frosting recipe without a fuss.

*"Melissa wants to bake cakes? Oh my, how sweet. Of course, she and her little friend can have the recipe. My pleasure."*

The coffee cake recipe we were interested in acquiring came from Helen's grandmother.

*"Here you go, dear. You girls have fun!"*

*"That's all we want to do, Grandma! Have fun! Thank you."*

Cake for breakfast! *Weeee....*

Finally, we nabbed a carrot cake recipe from the Hollands because it's important to eat your veggies! They were friends of my parents and in the doctor business, too. For years after happily handing over her carrot cake recipe, Sue Holland would cut recipes out of *The Boston Globe* and mail them to us. Boy, was she dedicated to the cause. (The illusion that carrot cake is healthy still runs rampant in the twenty-first century. I'm reminded of it by customers daily.)

Like our faraway kindred spirit, Susumu Kakinuma, who'd perfected just two types of pizza, we stopped at three cakes, figuring our collection covered most people's needs. Well, technically we had four, as the Chocolate Layer Cake came in a *His* (with nuts) & *Hers* (no nuts) versions. We'd roll in a cake of the month by spring, once we'd gotten the baking component of our baking business down.

Years later, I would learn that Bertha's triple-layer chocolate cake with the fudge frosting recipe—the cake that launched a thousand orders our first year—had come from the back of a chocolate baking bar she'd purchased from Kroger. This might have explained why she was so quick to give it up. But, back before Google, if someone gave you a book recommendation, a rave review of a new restaurant, or a homemade recipe for a kickass chocolate cake, you didn't pull out your smartphone to double-check the facts against Goodreads, Yelp, or AllRecipes.com. You smiled big and said thank you.

"*Thank you, Bertha! A million thanks.*"

Three days later, Helen asked, "What do we charge for the cakes?"

"We should research that," I said, tossing Helen the phonebook and picking up the phone.

Five minutes later, after calling three local bakeries and asking what they charged, we decided to go with the median of those prices: $15 per cake including delivery.

Four days later, we had the name of the business, the location for our startup (my condo), the names of the products we were going to sell, and the price including delivery. And, after shooting down the idea of "let's add a basket to my bike and deliver them that way," we decided to use our Hondas as the mode of cake transport for the time being.

This meant it was time to fork over some capital.

We did a quick tally of the money we'd need upfront. That list included ingredients to bake cakes, pans to bake the cakes in, and marketing materials. We contributed $250 each to the company kitty. We would never put in another dime until we needed a building loan in 1996 to expand.

Out of that capital, as we didn't have any cake orders because no one knew we existed, our first business expense was 250 plastic cake knives with *Piece of Cake* stamped on them, along with our phone number. At that point we didn't have a logo. But, by the following year, Helen's friend, Scott, who helped with advertising, came in one day with a flyer that had a logo on top, which he'd designed.

We use that logo to this day.

## Piece of Cake

Two weeks later, the box with the knives arrived. It was ominous in appearance. If a VW Bug were wound in bubble wrap and stuffed inside it, I wouldn't have been surprised. It felt that big to me at the time. I signed for it and dragged the box into my condo. That's when my adrenaline kicked in and I ripped into it, slicing through the top with a pair of scissors from my junk drawer. Then, I exhaled and pried open the box flaps. Staring back at me was a sea of white knives with our business info engraved in red. It was hypnotizing. Two hundred and fifty plastic cake knives looked like a supply that would last an eternity.

"I'm going to go to my grave with these knives," I said out loud to no one. Then, I imagined the wake. My stone-cold, stark-white nose sticking out through a pile of plastic *Piece of Cake* knives as they closed the casket. *"Melissa was a bright girl with a big future, but she never understood limits. What a loss."*

That's when Helen walked in after work and shook me from my nightmare.

"Whoa," she said on seeing the knives. "Well, they were cheap and they're more useful than a business card that's going to end up lost at the bottom of someone's purse."

At that, I smiled.

We did have plenty of funds left over for ingredients, pans, and measuring cups, enough to bake a hundred cakes. All we needed now were cake orders.

In the meantime....

# 5

## OUR ONLY PARTY WITHOUT CAKE

Friday, September 5, 1985 (to be exact), one month into our big business idea, we had four of the five steps complete in our business model:

1. Acquire recipes.
2. Figure out a price.
3. Throw in capital.
4. Order marketing materials.
5. Rally up some customers.

We needed to spread the word!

My father was an oral surgeon and my mother had turned her photography hobby into a career by the time we kids were grown. They had connections. Helen and I did, too, as I grew up here and she married a local. And it seemed that everyone we knew worked in the corporate world at a big company.

By the mid-to-late eighties, the economy was booming. Reaganomics played a big role in this, reducing government spending and lowering tax rates so people had more take-home income. People were making money and spending it, and big business was back with a vengeance, which was ultimately our target market. (Not that I investigated any of that then. I just thought it might be interesting to note for all you *business* people reading.)

## TIMING REALLY IS EVERYTHING

So, my mom and dad held a pre-grand-opening soirée at their house, and it was a real hit. We drank wine and asked everyone to *pretty please* grab a flyer on their way out and to *pretty, pretty please* put them up on their bulletin boards at work.

Then, we sat back and waited for business to roll in.

The lady we bought the plethora of plastic cake knives from became our first customer.

On that fine Monday morning on October 7, 1985, after our party, I had the first-day-of-work jitters. So, rather than stare at the mustard-yellow phone attached to my kitchen wall, willing it to ring, I took off for a bike ride through the Virginia-Highlands, a fun and trendy area in Downtown Atlanta. When I returned, my answering machine was blinking. Mom and Belinda called daily, so I wasn't getting my hopes too high when I hit *Play*.

But, on hearing the message, I danced with delight. "One triple-layer chocolate cake with fudge frosting coming right up!" Then, I called Helen at work. "We've got an order. We've got our first order!"

Then, I did the next natural thing, and went out to buy cake pans.

At Kroger is where I discovered that cake pans came in three sizes: 8", 10", and 12". Who knew? (Probably everyone but me. And Helen.) I hedged my bets, played the perimeters, and bought an 8" and 12".

On the way home, I stopped at a local bakery and asked them if I could purchase one of their white, cardboard cake boxes.

When I got home, I read the recipe. It called for 10" cake pans.

Bummer.

I reread the recipe, memorizing the ingredients, which was simple enough, and I mentally notated the part about "cooling racks."

Then, with my head hung low, I went back to Kroger for 10" cake pans. I also scooped up the ingredients for the chocolate cake.

When I returned home, I remembered I'd forgotten the cooling racks. *It's not like I forgot the eggs.* I assumed it'd be fine. Maybe the oven in my condo came with cooling racks...?

Then I cooked my first cake ever. Excuse me: I "baked" my first cake ever.

Removing it from the oven with my brand-new oven mitts, I flipped the pan and shook, so the cake could cool onto the counter.

As sad as it was to stare at all those broken chunks, it tasted fantastic. "Wow!" was the exact word I remembered uttering. This gave me the motivation to venture to Kroger a third time, where I was introduced to a cooling rack, which made sense, and then I cruised back home.

I baked another cake. It looked and smelled of perfection as I removed it from the oven. This time, I set the pan on the counter, jimmied around the cake and the edge of the pan with a butter knife, then turned the pan over, and gently shimmied the cake out onto the cooling rack.

Another bummer.

I baked a third cake. As I removed it in all its glorious perfection from the oven—at least I had that part down—I set the pan, right side up, on the cooling rack and walked away for fifteen minutes as instructed.

Fifteen long minutes later, I cautiously approached my creation. "Now be a nice cake and stay together for Melissa," I cooed.

The cake cooperated!

I did this routine two more times (three layers), then frosted it all. After that, I waited for Helen to get home, so she could box and bow it.

Three hours later, Helen arrived. She tasted one of the defective cake chunks. "Wow!" she said.

"I know!" I replied.

That was the entirety of the discussion about how the cake tasted. We had tasted them before, so we assumed they'd be great. Now, we knew that if we followed the recipes to a T, they'd always be "wow." This chocolate cake was so much better than the cakes we'd purchase from the bakeries downtown. The difference was shocking. All those cakes we'd settled for...all our lives...what were we thinking? This cake was the bomb. If you really think about it, we are all connoisseurs of cake. I couldn't believe it. She couldn't believe it. But it was true. We had a product that was better than anything we'd ever tried on anyone's birthday. Ever.

Then, I watched with a mixture of pride and joy as Helen placed the triple-layer chocolate cake in the white bakery box, affixed it with a multi-colored ribbon from my wrapping paper bin, and tucked one of our plastic *Piece of Cake* knives into the top of the box. Teamwork!

The next morning, I set out to deliver it.

When I handed it over to the plastic knife lady, she said, "It's so heavy."

I had no idea if that was good or bad, so I smiled and said, "Yup!" Then I jumped in my Honda and drove away like it was business as usual.

Belinda will forever be credited with ordering Cake #2. God bless family. She "phoned" it in from my living room couch. She was too pregnant to do much else that fall, except sit around and keep me company, waiting for labor to kick in. Maybe she felt bad that people weren't busting down our door. Maybe she was craving cake. Anyway, Belinda ordered a carrot cake, keeping it on the healthy side for the baby.

Shortly thereafter, she gave birth. We delivered a carrot cake to the hospital, too, in celebration of Kendrick.

And then, business was off and running, if at a modest pace.

In the mornings, I'd deliver the order (sometimes it would be "orders" plural) from the day before. Then, I'd hopefully come home to a message or I'd wait for one to come in and bake that cake, getting it ready for the next morning.

Helen would show up after work and frost the cake (or cakes) I'd made, then box and bow 'em. We always worked as a team, even in the early days when only one of us was needed to keep the business afloat.

By mid-November, one month in, once the orders had doubled from two to four, the business grew more steadily.

In early December, thanks to my dad's free marketing, we got our first Christmas order for fifteen cakes. It was huge! It was also an indication that the holidays were going to be peak cake-ordering season and we'd better keep our cooling rack at the ready. (Actually, we'd better buy more!) Fifteen cakes: that was forty-five layers of cake to bake, cool, stack into triple layers, then frost, box and bow, and deliver. Fifteen cake boxes take up the whole back seat of a 1982, four-door Honda Accord, by the way.

*They look glorious back there*, I thought, as Helen and I took off, nice and easy, from the parking lot of Cross Creek Condos on the afternoon of December 18, 1985 to deliver our cakes to their first corporate Christmas party.

o o o

Today, every *Piece of Cake* cake is delivered with a plastic cake knife tucked in the top of the box. The knives are now ordered in lots of 50,000—and they are everywhere. You can find one in the breakroom junk drawer of almost any office in Atlanta and in thousands of homes.

# 6

## BUILDING THE BUSINESS, ONE OVEN RACK AT A TIME

People look at you differently when you're an outlier. I didn't know this until I became one, as I had never done anything prior to launching POC that would've taken my family or friends by surprise. I was a real follower, since I'd been a kid. I was never dramatic or rebellious or emotional, even in my teens, not even for a minute. My parents were the authority figures and what they said was gospel. Life is much different these days. I have two teenagers, so I can attest to this firsthand. They are my focus, to a fault some days. But, back in the sixties and seventies, children were an accessory. My parents had full, rich lives and we were but cogs in their wheels.

Back when I was growing up, I did as I was told. I ate what I was served. I had responsibilities, my parents were big on that, but I always met them. We all did. I made goals (of which they either helped to create or condoned) and attained them. But I certainly didn't do any of this consciously. My parents had never laid out rules or a plan. I just seemed to instinctually know what to do and, without effort, followed protocol. Even with Piece of Cake, yes, I knew we'd have success, but we are not the MBA protégé. We've never had a business plan, and I've never laid out any rules. We've all just moved forward with an innate understanding of the process and respect for it. Those who didn't, simply didn't stick around.

There wasn't a single incident in my life until the launching of Piece of Cake where I'd taken anyone by surprise. I didn't feel like one of the pack on the inside, but I had fallen into step naturally enough to appear as if I were. And, I'd never attracted attention to myself in the way that intellectual, witty, defiant, or boisterous people do. While I achieved my goals, I wasn't an overachiever, so I didn't stand out in that way, either. I had never learned (or gotten up the courage) to do things my way throughout my formative years.

For years, though, after I'd checked all obligatory duties off my kid list and was given my adult card, I was in a state of constant, low-grade meditation, even though that word *meditation* didn't exist yet, at least not in Atlanta, at least not in the eighties. Going from traditional Melissa, a quiet and dutiful member of the pack, to *The Cake Lady* was a shock for people, a real outlier kind of move.

But my mom got it. She'd started a career at forty without thinking twice. So in tune with me was she, that, within days of our announcement, she waltzed into my condo with her Mixmaster in tow. This was a gift for her wedding in 1952, and something she used but once a year to make her "special" cheesecake for Thanksgiving. "You're going to need this more than I do, Melissa." A truer statement had never been uttered. That Mixmaster got us through our first two years. It sits on display in my office to this day.

The women in my family didn't believe in boundaries.

By the fall of 1986, having long since outgrown the one oven in my kitchen a year into this undertaking, our neighbor was kind enough to let us use her oven while she was at work, and I'd rewired my sunporch to accommodate two ovens. Both were purchased from Goodwill. Actually, one of them might have been sitting on the side of the road near Goodwill. That made the business 18 percent more efficient and assuaged our daily anxiety by about—*let's slide that decimal point over*—1.8 percent, which was better than nothing.

Giant bags of flour and sugar lined the walls of my living room. My fridge consisted of beverages on the top shelf (milk for the recipes and a few cocktails), butter lined the next shelf, and eggs were everywhere else. Cakes cooled on every available flat surface of my apartment, including the tops of lampshades. Who knew how idyllic those would turn out to be? Certainly not the lampshade makers or they'd have been cross marketing. My dog, Moe, became so accustomed to the frenetic level of activity, she no longer looked up or even shifted positions when someone walked in the door. *So much for a guard dog. Might need to invest in an alarm system.* My new décor, a plethora of baked *and unbaked* goods, actually served as a natural deterrent for criminals et. al, so, I guess no alarm system was needed. Even some of my gentlemen callers would start out intrigued by my business endeavor and entrepreneurial spirit, but then grow bored and confused. I wasn't trading on Wall Street or slinking into a one-piece-female-race-car-driver jumpsuit and hitting the track. I mean, I was covered in flour and cracking eggs all day. No one was commenting on my flashy work uniform. No one was suggesting we were on our way to becoming the millionaires next door. No one perceived Piece of Cake as avant-garde. There was nothing sexy about this gig. And, at a glance, it didn't scream success. I didn't mind so much. I was so invested in the company that everything else took a back seat. Well, everything else wound up in the trunk, as the cakes were in the back seat.

Right about this time, with my pre-holiday adrenaline kicking in, I ran into a woman I'd met back when I was doing volunteer work at a family crisis center. My parents were small on free time and big on volunteering, and there were only so many bike rides a girl could take, so I found a local nonprofit and rolled up my sleeves. Anyway, all the women there, from employees to volunteers to victims of domestic violence and financial hardship, were so curious about our cakes. Our cakes did not discriminate! But I didn't have a lot of answers back then, as I was a novice business owner and cake baker. Well, I had answers now, some thirteen months later.

The questions came rolling at me.

This woman was so glad to hear the business was off the ground that she suggested I contact her husband. He owned a local printing firm. "Just go in there, Melissa, and say hi. Tell him I sent you and that your cakes are delightful, the perfect Christmas gift."

So, with a handwritten greeting on a piece of notebook paper, I ran into his building, plopped the cake and note on his secretary's desk, and basically skedaddled. Self-promotion has never been my strong suit.

> *Dear Mr. So 'n' So,*
>
> *I recently ran into your wife. I have started this cake baking and delivery business. She told me to tell you about it. And here's a cake. I hope you like it. They make great gifts. Thank you for your time.*
>
> *Melissa Bunnen*

He called a few days later and ordered 100 cakes to send to all his clients. His clients were law firms, advertising agencies, and brokerage firms all over Atlanta.

And, just like that, we were on everyone's radar.

## FEEL THE FEAR AND BAKE IT ANYWAY

We deliver cakes to these businesses to this day. I owe a lot to him. We were able to walk our product into 100 successful businesses, and we didn't pay a dime for marketing. Well, we sacrificed a cake, so I guess it cost us a few bucks' worth of ingredients. It was serendipitous.

Suddenly, business was snowballing.

# 7

## CAKE-MAKING ZOMBIES

About three weeks before Christmas is when it hit us: we were in trouble, big trouble. We had agreed to bake 100 cakes in my pipsqueak condo kitchen with its 3.5 ovens. We already knew we'd be spending four or five weeks working late hours to get through the marathon that is the Christmas season, but, with the big order on top of the regular holiday orders, it felt like we'd have to start running a marathon a day in the form of 400, 100-meter sprints to keep up with the bake load and deliver the cakes on schedule. Yes, we knew we weren't facing a life or death situation. I mean, we had our wits about us, but people take the holidays seriously. And our word was as good as gold. If you ordered a cake, barring the apocalypse, you were getting your cake in one piece and on time.

To make things more challenging, interesting, nightmarish, what have you, Mr. So 'n' So wanted every cake to come with a carton of orange juice—they were all coffee cakes. With no room left in either of our fridges or the neighbor's for more than a quart or two of OJ, we'd have to buy them on the fly as we delivered the cakes. I don't know how I let him rope us into that part. It was such a hassle. Looking back, however, thank goodness he didn't ask for something really obscure. I'm sure I would've agreed to pull whatever out of my...hat.

*"You want us to deliver each cake dressed like elves while riding in a horse-drawn sleigh? Sure!"*

*"Sing 'Jingle Bells' on delivery? No problem!"*

*"Can I play the ukulele? I'm sure I can learn. How hard can it be?"*

I'm kidding. I would not have done any of that. (Helen might have....)

We were both going on five hours of sleep on a good night. Helen had finally quit her job, so she could devote all her time to Piece of Cake. I don't even recall if she put in two weeks' notice, probably more like two hours' notice. We got that crazed that fast. And, by the way, 78 steps were a lot of steps after a night of caking, knowing that, at six a.m., you'd be en route back for another day of endless caking.

Helen once said in an interview: *"All I remember in year two is being up until three a.m., walking back across the parking lot, getting three hours of sleep, and being back at Melissa's by dawn."*

We were cake-making zombies, all dead in the eyes, but, instead of blood and guts, we were dripping in cake bits. And slowing down was not an option; we couldn't lose our momentum; the reputation of our young company was at stake.

Christmas #2 was going to make us or break us.

Then, at dawn of day two of the big order, while I was ear high in eggshells with sixty cakes down and forty to go, Dave called and said, "Melissa, Helen can't come over. I think she had a nervous breakdown. Or cakedown. Or something."

I could hear Helen in the background. She'd screech then whimper like she was being flogged. At one point, I swore I heard her speaking in tongues. But then I realized I was probably just hallucinating.

"Oh, yes, she can!" I told Dave. "Tell her to get her butt over here. Now!"

I noticed my hand was shaking a little when I put the phone back on the receiver. *Is my sugar low? High? When's the last time I ate?* "Pull it together, Melissa," I said under my breath. If Helen, the most even-keeled person in the world, was having a nervous cakedown, my nervous cakedown would have to get in line.

I grabbed a carton of OJ, pried it open, and took a gulp. I'd pay for that later with an extra stop at the grocery store but, for now, I felt more normalized.

That's when Helen walked through the door. Her eyes were puffy as hell. But she'd pulled herself together enough to make the 78-step trek back to the "office." And she'd dressed in real clothes. Even if she'd skipped a hole while buttoning her blouse, she wasn't in her pajamas. Go Helen.

But I knew we needed to make some changes. Can't have half the company in the midst of mental collapse. So, after popping four cakes in each of my ovens (don't forget the neighbor's!), I took Moe for a walk so I could clear my head and meditate on everything.

It was on that brisk-morning jaunt in early December that it dawned on me. One year and change into the business—

*brace yourselves for this one*—that I could put more than one cake into each oven at a time. This lightbulb moment made me feel as if I were the creator of the light itself.

No, it did not.

Well, maybe not light, but I felt like the creator of electricity.

No, I did not.

It felt like I was neither the creator of light nor electricity. I was more the guy who was given a lamp, a lightbulb, and an outlet for Christmas...and it took me a year and two months to figure out how to screw the lightbulb into the lamp and plug the lamp into the outlet. It was embarrassing beyond words.

I felt my entire body go crimson, like I was blushing from my cheekbones to my toes. *Bill and Ted's Excellent Adventure* wouldn't hit the big screen for another year, but if it had, the conversation I would have had with Helen on my return with Moe would've gone something like this:

"Dude," I'd say, "we can put, like, more than one cake in each oven."

And, after the longest beat in history, Helen would respond, "Whoa."

SOMETIMES, THE MOST OBVIOUS SOLUTION IS *THE MOST OBVIOUS SOLUTION*

# 8

## WELCOME TO THE BLACK HOLE

By packing each oven with multiple cakes simultaneously, we became four times as efficient overnight. (The extra baking racks helped. Thank goodness that "*haha*" moment came on the heels of the former). With this revelation, half the staff (*aka* the other president) was spared insanity. We had stumbled upon the first "innovation" that had a tremendous impact on the volume we could handle. The only reason I mention this here is because I'd already confessed to it in print a couple decades back: "*I mean, I'm not proud of how long it took us to figure out that we could put more than one cake in the oven at a time, but, when we did, it was really big.*"

Next: We had to move from creative mode to business mode. It was the only way to survive and thrive at that point, and that much we knew.

Our next "innovations" went by the names of Jennifer and Donna. They became POC's first two paid employees. (Note to Millennials: Back in the eighties, the acronym "POC" [person of color] hadn't yet surfaced. It was ours for the taking, as being PC wouldn't be on anyone's radar until well into the twenty-first century.)

Both women were family friends. Donna worked with Dave at the law firm, and Jennifer was still in high school. But we needed people to box and deliver cakes, like, yesterday. So, when we ran into them at an early-in-the-season Christmas party, we asked if they wanted to help us through the holiday madness. We probably didn't even ask them. We likely gave a general shout-out and they were within earshot.

"When do you need us?"

"Whenever you'd like to come in."

"How often?"

"As often as you'd like."

That was the long 'n' short of both the interview *and* training process.

They'd show up when they could. In Jennifer's case, that was after bio class. Donna would come after she'd finished up at her corporate day job. On Fridays or whatever day they'd think to ask, I'd write them a check. I'm pretty sure it was a check. Sometimes, it was cash, depending on the amount of baking going on that day. They made five bucks an hour, not a glorified salary but it was above minimum wage. Not bad for a side job where you made your own hours and got paid by the honor system.

Even before we'd ever hired a soul, our theory was if we could lure them into the POC black hole, they wouldn't be able to get out. We were proof of that. We were trapped in the vortex! This airtight plan, this scheme, this theory turned "law" in no time, and, thus, our system—of not hiring but somehow acquiring employees that worked hard and remained loyal—was born. This management style would get us through the remainder of the twentieth century and the first decade of the twenty-first.

No joke.

Jennifer's two sisters would start coming to work, as well. They were in college, wanted a few extra dollars, and thought it looked like Jen was having fun, the kind of fun they wanted in on. So many people wanted to help during Christmastime and summer break. And we didn't turn any helping hands away. All these cute boys would come, and all the cute girls would follow. Teenage hormones alone got POC through the holidays for many, many years.

# 9

## TOMATO SOUP CAKE, ANYONE?

Now business-minded, we started making decisions that seemed nutty to a lot of people but kept us sane and moving in a forward direction with limited stress.

For example, neither one of us could write "*Happy Birthday, So 'n' So*" on our cakes with any effectiveness. The cakes were really starting to take shape, but when we attempted to personalize them, they'd revert to looking like something a six-year-old made for their mom. Inscription was not our forte. We decided to declare, like rebels, that our cakes would be unadorned. We'd add pecans or crushed walnuts to the tops no problem, but we flat-out refused to blemish them with unnecessary birthday wishes.

"*Our cakes are different.*"

"*Our cakes are special.*"

"*Our cakes are not like the other cakes. They cannot be pigeon-holed.*"

*"Our cakes are too good for little, old words!"* (I did not tell anyone that.)

The result was the POC cakes took on a very different look from the run-of-the-mill bakery or supermarket cakes, and they became, in fact, special.

This homemade simplicity has become part of the panache of Piece of Cake and was probably key in the tremendous growth of the business that would take place over the next decade.

Shortly thereafter, we started featuring a cake of the month. For example, Red Velvet Cake has become the standard in February. Though I am not a coconut kind of person, we eventually rolled Coconut Cake into one of the holiday months instead of fruit cake. (Just say no to fruit cake! You know, there's really only one and it travels around the world.)

But, because of the extreme pace with which the business was taking off, we couldn't think beyond that. We never had a business plan. I still don't. I just keep doing what feels right and not committing to any new endeavors that don't...feel right.

We came out the other end of our second Christmas with the company knowing one thing for certain: there was no turning back now.

∘ ∘ ∘

Being our first and biggest supporter was never enough for my mother. She wanted to contribute in some significant way to the company. For that reason, she'd been pushing her tomato soup cake recipe on us since my sales doubled from two to four. We'd obtained all our recipes from family and friends, so it was understandable that she wanted in on fun (fame), especially being one of the boss's moms. The truth was I'd gotten my "natural baking skills" from my mother. It wasn't likely she could contribute anything beyond sideline applause. Her rolodex of recipes was basically an envelope shoved under some oven mitts in the skinny drawer next to the stove. She kept calling the tomato soup cake one her "special" recipe to entice me. But, with her library of recipes totaling around five, they were all special.

The tomato soup cake recipe called for sugar, eggs, flour, butter, salt, cinnamon, nutmeg, mix this with that and blend. It started out pretty standard, then it got interesting: add raisins, chopped carrots, and a cup of tomato soup in lieu of milk. Bake at 350° for an hour.

*What?*

Re-reading the recipe, I could taste the, um, tomato soup, coming up in the back of my throat. It was original, which was her angle. I considered renaming it. Tomatoes were a fruit, after all: *The Other Fruit Cake.* But, even with rebranding—*A Fruit Cake for the Modern Fruit Cake Lover*—I couldn't bring myself to add a can of tomato soup to a beautiful bowl of cake batter. I just couldn't do it.

This didn't create a chasm between Mom and me so much as give her a mission.

Shortly after the holidays, one of our dogs died. Mom is a lover of animals but especially dingoes, the wild Australian dogs. And, she always believed, as with people, that dogs should have companions. So, off she went to a breeder in South Carolina to find a new dingo to go with our remaining dingo, Eddie. There, she got into a conversation about Piece of Cake with the breeder.

"My daughter started a company and she bakes these wonderful cakes and—" and, no sooner did the word "cake" escape her lips than the dingo breeder ran into her house and came back with a recipe scratched across a piece of notebook paper.

"Here, give her this! It's my white chocolate cake recipe. It's amazing!"

"Will do!" Lucinda said, dingo pup in one hand, white chocolate cake recipe in the other.

Mom came back all excited. She now had another dingo, Elfina, and this recipe, the one that was going to launch POC into the stratosphere of success based on the dingo breeder's review. Well, when someone shoves a tomato soup cake recipe at you for years, there's a recovery period before you dive into their Great Idea Number #2. I put the white chocolate cake recipe in a drawer to let it hibernate for the winter.

I kept circling back in my head, though, as white chocolate cake had a certain *je ne sais quoi* about it. Mostly, it sounded normal. I could sell white chocolate cake, no rebranding necessary. Well, summer rolled around and we had some down time.

*Why not?* I thought one day.

I pulled the recipe out of a desk drawer, gathered the ingredients, and baked the cake.

Two hours later, Helen walked in.

"So, what do you think?"

"Wow," she said on tasting it.

"I know, right?" I replied, taking another bite.

"Is their white chocolate melted right—"

"—into the batter, just like with our chocolate layer cake."

"Wow."

"I know, right? Wow."

And that was that. We had a fourth cake on the short list of regular menu items.

## LISTEN TO YOUR MOTHER (MOST OF THE TIME)

The following year, White Chocolate Cake became our number one seller. It's been holding steady there for thirty-three years and counting.

# 10

## DOES THIS THING HAVE AN OFF SWITCH?

One can trip over heaping sacks of flour in their living room for only so long before considering leasing actual business space for one's growing business.

What's funny to me is that so many people work from home nowadays, but when I look back on us doing it, it seemed nuts. I hear friends talk about the perks and challenges of having a home business all the time. The number one perk is flexibility. If you have a family, you can manage your children's lives and the family schedules more easily. The downside is you're "always at work." There's no off switch. It can feel like one long workday with no beginning, no end, plenty of chauffeuring, and a few loads of laundry in between. Today more than ever, people understand that. A lot of people have home offices, which helps to separate business from family life. I have one now, too. But, imagine your entire home is your office. (I know a lot of you understand that, too.) The only room in my condo that was truly free of cake paraphernalia was the bathroom. Remember the two ovens on my sunporch? So much for relaxing with a cup of coffee out there on a lazy Sunday morning, as it was always above ninety-five degrees. When you work from home, there is always something that needs to be done. There is really no relaxing. Of course, at the time, I couldn't have relaxed if I'd wanted to.

And, even more than becoming an instant outlier by starting a company with a product of which we weren't familiar, in the eighties, working from home wasn't cool. The situation was just plain odd. People thought I was nuts for good reason.

But we were in our Piece of Cake vortex, spinning out of control but managing. We welcomed the joiners, Donna and Jennifer, even though more people meant less wiggle room in our pint-sized factory. We couldn't keep it up. It was too intense. The safety of it all, the proverbial sameness, was comforting, and the rent was more than reasonable. But those comforts had worn thin.

I was terrified to commit to a space we'd have to pay for every single month. Part of me thought that an official workspace would make the business too real. I wasn't oblivious to the fortuitous timing of it all. We had created a business and product that attracted people. Facts. But we were two crazy twenty-somethings running amok in Corporate America. We were making our own hours; there was no dress code; and, we didn't even have a license to run a business from my condo. (That part was not our fault.)

When we'd gone to the license bureau to buy one, they chuckled. I'm not kidding. When we told the clerk we wanted to bake cakes and deliver them, she and the rest of the staff thought it was adorable. Then she said they'd sold a slew of licenses recently for home businesses and told us to go have fun. "Enjoy yourselves, ladies. Don't worry about a silly, old license." We'd heard someone mumble something about the gargantuan rate of failure for home businesses in between all the well wishes.

And that was that. We left empty-handed but with a strong verbal blessing from the state.

How long could we keep this up? Running amok and making money? Did our wild idea have an expiration date? I couldn't imagine it, as failing never occurred to me. But, the cushion of running POC out of my condo made for a good night's sleep, you know, on the nights when we weren't baking till the bars closed and waking when the donut shops opened.

Making the business official by giving it a home sounded like an exciting step toward success, but it also felt like a lot of pressure. We'd for sure have to pay for a license now, and an inspection. If you don't count the basics, which were pots, pans, ingredients, and the two secondhand ovens (that were practically free), we hadn't poured any money into the company. It was freeing to work without overhead. The biggest risk we'd taken by that point was Helen quitting her day job. We didn't have "real" employees, and we were paying ourselves next to nothing, and sometimes nothing at all.

I was nonplussed by the twenty-hour workdays. What I wouldn't give for some of that twenty-seven-year-old energy now. The fact that my condo had turned into a cake-baking factory didn't bother me a bit, either, despite the looks I'd get from visitors. And Moe was fine. But, we'd both gotten several talkings to by our condo association (Helen and me, not the dog and me). It's not like people were picking up cakes—we were a gated community—so we weren't constantly adding names to the visitor list at the gate. But, we were coming and going, my silver Honda and her blue one, about thirty times a day. There was no law against that. We knew this for a fact, as we'd asked Dave to read the fine print in the association bylaws. Still, the neighbors, those that weren't entertained by our goings on, felt attacked by the mania. Not to mention the trash can, which happened to be right outside the back of my place, was overflowing with garbage all the time now. It was a junkyard of discarded cake boxes, eggshells, egg cartons, milk cartons, flour bags, etc. (That vision stayed with me and got me into the habit of recycling to this very day.) And, I had the other prez to consider. Helen was a married woman, a certified adult, and she needed to be taken seriously. She was also pregnant with her first child. More than anything, she deserved the little bit of leg room my condo could no longer provide. Plus, wow, was it hot in there. It wasn't just the sunporch. The ovens were on long hours every week. The whole place was a real sweat lodge.

Our tiny business was growing steadily, and we'd been able to save up thanks to our startup location. Every spare penny was put into an account in anticipation of this day. That safety net of cash, around ten thousand dollars, gave me comfort. But I wanted it to grow. Having a supply, a rainy-day backup, not only put my mind at ease, it gave me confidence. Was I ready to go with the flow and plunge into the next phase? We had always been united when it came to building the business through hard work and spending conservatively, and she was ready. I guess that meant I was, too. (C'mon, you knew POC was a woman. She was my ship and, I, her dutiful navigator.)

I read *Shoe Dog* not too long ago, the memoir by Nike Founder Phil Knight. I know, I know, POC is not a Nike empire, but Phil Knight was a regular guy with a big dream once upon a time. In *Shoe Dog*, he talked about how, in the early days, back when he was importing Tigers from Japan, he poured all profits into purchasing more tennis shoes whenever he'd sell out. He'd have to go to the bank and ask for a loan that was double the last loan. He'd duke it out with the bank manager every time, as they did not agree with his approach. The bank's stance was that it wasn't good business practice to use all your savings to continually double down on your young business. It was high risk beyond belief. Well, having forgone the part about learning how to bake a cake before launching a cake baking business, we hadn't lost touch with how to grow the business in the safest manner possible. Phil Knight gambled repeatedly and won. But I was terrified of spending money the company had been accumulating since the sale of our first Chocolate Layer Cake with Chocolate Frosting. And, so, there it sat, safely at First Atlanta, gaining three percent interest for the last few years.

But all those emotional issues attached to the imminent move, as grand as they were, paled compared to the logistical quandary I was in.

We were so frantic baking cakes night and day that we had absolutely no time to deal with a move. *How does one grow a business when one has no time to devote to growing the business because one's time is filled with running the business?* That tongue twister, the question of the century, ran through my brain hourly.

Fifty percent of small businesses fail within five years; 90 percent by ten. I knew that much and didn't want to become a statistic. No one opens a business to become part of the majority, to become a sad memory. How could we prevent that from becoming POC's future? The business was moving at an impressive pace, managing our lives more than the other way around. POC wanted more of our time, more of our devotion. She wanted us to crack more eggs and fast, to no end. That, more than anything, had me paralyzed or in denial about taking time out to move. So much for getting out of the nine-to-five grind. Now we were working five to nine, with three hours to sleep and three to worry, then back to cracking eggs.

In the end, I figured I'd better listen to what the business was telling me. And, more than anything, Piece of Cake wanted to grow.

If you don't listen to your intuition and go with the flow, you can't (here comes another Cake-ism):

## GROW WITH THE FLOW

# 11

## "WHEN YOU COME TO A FORK IN THE ROAD, TAKE IT."

Right after Christmas, we started looking for space. This was when Helen's sister, Margaret, said the printing company she used for all her business needs was relocating. They needed to expand just like us. She thought their space would be the perfect next step. Having been inside our current location on more than one occasion, Margaret had acquired enough intel to know what kind of space Piece of Cake would need to stretch her cooling racks out in.

So, we went to see this space at 1985 Howell Mill Road in an oddball area of Atlanta sandwiched between the tiny neighborhoods of Buckhead and industrial landmarks like the Coca-Cola plant and the Railroad Yard.

It was a tired-looking area in need of life. It was a safe enough neighborhood, though. No one was disputing that. It just hadn't been discovered yet. Today, it's a business mecca, bustle here, there, everywhere. And, it's got real curb appeal. Back then, in '89, the indoor-outdoor pizzeria was a car repair shop. Margaret's business, one of a couple gift shops she owned, was next to that. And the bank that's now catty-corner from the pizzeria was a Mexican restaurant called US Bar y Grill. Margaritas, margaritas, margaritas would soon become our drink of choice. This was awesome right up until the day all their furniture ended up on the street, as the building was being seized in exchange for back taxes. And, *poof,* just like that they were gone. No more margaritas by the pitcher to get us through the holidays. And, Dr. Dinwald, our landlord, had a chiropractic practice upstairs. He'd end up coming down regularly with some tongue-in-cheek words of wisdom:

> *"If you need me, I've got your 'back.'"*
> *"I can adjust everything but your personality!"*
> *"I might crack you up, but I can crack you down, too."*

TV repairman Carl Chin, in the lower level of the building, had words of wisdom, too: "All I want to do is repair TVs." He must have said that a thousand times. I remember thinking, *I wonder what my mantra is?* I don't want to just bake cakes, that I knew. One day, Carl got offered a contract with a hotel chain, but he had to hire a staff and deal with tons of contracts. He did not manifest his dream of working solo and focusing on the TV repair part of his business. I took this as a warning to be careful about what I wished for, and to be open to possibilities if I didn't have a singular vision.

Upstairs, there was a seamstress of questionable mental stability, a friendly printer who hung around our backdoor on his smoke breaks (we do business with him to this day), and a barbershop run by a father-son team. The father suffered an unfortunate death from a penile implant—no joke—shortly after we arrived. So, the son had to take over. He was trying to patent animal skin swimsuits for men on the side from trimming hair and shaving beards. He'd come down with a new model periodically. "How do you feel about zebra? Panther? Snakeskin?" They all looked the same to me: wrong.

The Howell Mill venue was 800 square feet of dingy basement space with poor heating and air conditioning, archaic plumbing, and limited aesthetic appeal. It was so funky, it even smelled funky, but we loved it! Curb appeal aside, it was a giant step up from our current "factory location," with four times the cooking space. And an industrial-sized hose with a bleach-water solution had the place sparkling in no time. Rent was around $500 a month because this wasn't a storefront locale.

Margaret mentioned that she wanted to use part of our space for storage. This was fantastic, as she paid us a percentage of the rent in exchange for a little space.

Nobody was going to find Piece of Cake if they weren't intentionally given directions right to it. We were in the back, in the basement. You never really think about what's behind the storefront. This was ideal, too. We didn't want people nosing around our operation. The whole deal was we came to you. One of our future drivers would have this car that wouldn't go in reverse and, when she'd park in the back there, she could hardly ever get out. That's how tucked away we were. Our parking area was basically a tiny, dark cavernous space or, as we liked to call it: the entrance to the black hole. We were just a mile from our condos, though. So, we were in town, but with the capability of maintaining a downlow status till we could run the business like a well-oiled machine, or like a cake mixer on steroids, as we liked to say.

Then and Now: Mom's 1952 Mixmaster and our Mixers today

We had to sign a three-year lease. That was a huge commitment, but we were dedicated, well, more like hopelessly devoted. The business had taken off and we knew it was going to work. We signed on the dotted line. *Now it really has to work.*

Thank goodness for January after the holiday rush. It gave us time to pack and move. This used to be our slowest month, what with everyone making New Year's resolutions not to eat things like cake. *Grrr.* It's not like that anymore. We no longer feel the hit from any resolutions. Cake is the staple in most celebrations and will be till the end of time. *Ooh, that should be my mantra.* "Why worry later when you can worry now." *That's actually my mantra.*

Our first order of business was to have the space inspected. The Department of Agriculture sent over a guy.

He was young and very helpful at steering us in the right direction so there weren't any do-overs...and we cleared inspection. He called and came by a lot after the initial look-over. He said it was to check up on us, nice, young, enthusiastic inspector that he was. And, whenever he'd come by, he'd get a complimentary piece of whatever got cut that day because it (ironically) didn't make the cut. He was the inspector and I sure wasn't going to do anything to irk him. But after a while, I said to Helen, "That guy's got the biggest sweet tooth of anybody I know." She gave me a look and said, "It's not his dang sweet tooth that keeps pointing him in our direction, Melissa."

Not wanting any debt, we'd priced out industrial equipment beforehand: ovens, mixers, sinks, and tables. By the time we redid the floors and fixed the plumbing, we were just on the right side of zero. It was design on a dime, but it had to happen. We did not overspend. I cannot emphasize this enough. Over the years, whenever we've needed another oven or anything, we would always check the account and budget according to the available cash.

## EVERY DAY IS BLACK FRIDAY AT PIECE OF CAKE

Paying ourselves hadn't become a thing yet. We would have been lucky to have been making $5 an hour. We'd go as long as we could without a paycheck, until one of us would bring it up in the form of half-question, which would lead to a string of sentence fragments. Talking about taking money out of the company was all kinds of uncomfortable.

"Hey, when's the last time we...?"

"Did the thing with the money?"

"I dunno, like, three...?"

"Weeks?"

"Months," we'd say in unison.

"Time sure flies—"

"—when you're cracking eggs."

When we were bold enough to cut ourselves a check, it was for $500 just to stay afloat: mortgage, utility bills, dog food, and a couple cocktails on Saturdays. I was still in my twenties, after all, so that's where my money went.

# 12

## MAMA BEARS LOVE THEIR CUBCAKES

Melinda and Nancy were our first official employees at Howell Mill Road. They came aboard ready for the Valentine's Day rush. We sold red velvet cakes like crazy that February. The timing was perfect—new place, additional sets of hands, love was in the air. That year gave us insight that Valentine's cakes were going to be in high demand. US Bar y Grill would start selling us margaritas by the jug to keep my staff happy through the night hours on the thirteenth of February. Those tangy treats assuaged many a tear over the following years.

Melinda was the fastest box maker in town. At least that's what we kept telling her. If you compliment people, they'll enjoy the work more. Boy, was she an all-star box maker.

### NEVER UNDERESTIMATE THE POWER OF A COMPLIMENT

Nancy was young and married, too, like Helen. And she knew how to bake! We found this out at one of our social gatherings. In fact, Nancy knew all the tricks. "You don't have to peel the carrots, ladies, just chop 'em." Can you imagine the time we've saved over the years from just that one little tip? We obviously had to hire Nancy on the heels of that declaration.

She came to work her first day in a chef's coat. Helen and I doubled over laughing. "Oh, my God, that girl is official." Our Southern accents were in full force that morning as the commentary just kept rolling. That didn't stop Nancy. She showed up on day two in her chef's coat, as well. It did make a lot of sense, we deduced, even though she looked excessively official for POC.

On the flip side, that chef's coat made Piece of Cake look official, too. I mean, as CEOs and managers and Cakers and delivery women and jacks-of-all-trades, we didn't have any costumes distinguishing us as experts. Nancy looked great and no one mistook her for the janitor after hours like they would me, broom in my hands, cake dust on my cheeks. Nancy and her cake costume commanded respect. "Damn, does Nancy look cake-ish in that coat," we'd start commenting. Still, Nancy was only in charge of mixing the batter we'd created and putting the cakes in the oven. Come to think of it, she also made the chocolate frosting for the *His & Hers* chocolate layer cakes.

Nancy was the best frosting maker we'd ever seen. Making frosting was a tedious pain in the butt. Our frosting was thick and involved so much stirring, break-a-sweat kind of mixing. Anyone could do it, but we made sure Nancy knew her frosting was superior, so she'd want to make it for us daily. Go Nancy.

Despite the changes, we were afraid to let go too much, even though we made the leap to Howell Mill and were paying rent. We had our two employees for side tasks, but we needed ten. And we needed more people in the warzone baking cakes.

But, because of those crazy odds, we were able to start collecting paychecks every week. That was a nice change. We could pay ourselves—the upside to having one quarter the staff we actually needed! That had to be why we'd resisted hiring more people for so long. We struggled through it, doing everything ourselves. The issue had to be that we were both the good cops. Or the bad cops, not sure which, but there was no balance. We were both the cop that was conservative and wanted to keep the bank account for POC growing moderately. Neither of us was testing the other. We both just worked ourselves to the bones and didn't spend a dime of company money on anything frivolous. We got along great and were open to wearing any hat POC needed to keep running in a timely fashion. And, we were both willing to sacrifice our sanity to ensure that happened. Unfortunately, no one was the voice of reason or rationality.

My vision had been different back in the fall of '85, of course. I imagined myself walking from room to room with elegant authority, as if I were balancing an imaginary book on my head, checking in on the vast POC empire of employees, asking: "*Everything okay in here? Everything okay in here? Everything okay in here? ...It is? ...Oh, excellent.*"

The big surprise? I was in before dawn sifting flour. Every day. Even after we hired a few people, the lion's share of the baking was still on our shoulders. Poor Nancy in her starched and pressed chef's coat. She was allowed to tell us what to do and stir the batter and shove those cakes in the oven and make the frosting, but we drew the line after that.

"*We sort of hovered over those recipes,*" Helen said once in an interview. "*Other people could wrap them. We just had to crack the eggs and bake the cakes and they could do the rest.*"

It was true. We hovered like mama bears over our *cub*cakes. What were we protecting? Why did we have to be the ones to prepare all the cake batter and watch them bake? Yes, the cakes were the reason we were on a roll. But they all came with recipes because we didn't know anything about baking when we began the company. It stands to reason, therefore, that anyone could read the recipe and, if followed, the cake would turn out.

Did Susumu have this problem?

Was he up before dawn tossing circles of doughy pizza crust into the air wishing someone else was capable of the task but too paranoid or controlling or imbecilic to give another person a chance?

*How long can this go on?* I'd ask myself that question over and over. I s'pose my partner in cakes was asking herself the same thing.

It went on for far too long. Gluttons for punishment is all I can figure.

# 13

## OVEN RACK EPIPHANY 2.0

By summer, and despite Melinda and Nancy's special talents, Piece of Cake was, once again, eclipsing everything else in our lives.

One morning while on deliveries, I stopped at my dentist's office to have a crown replaced. It was a scheduled appointment. Well, someone lost track of time (and it wasn't me). You know how relaxing a visit to the dentist can be. (No? Just me?) Anyway, at some point I glanced at my watch. That's when I leaped out of the chair with gauze hanging out of my mouth and made a beeline for the door with an "I'll thee thack!" I had to deliver these certain cakes at a specific time that morning because I'd promised the customer, and I was taught never to go back on my word.

○ ○ ○

While it was nice having my home back—I could see my kitchen counter, I wasn't hopscotching over cake boxes in the

living room, and my sunporch was down to a balmy but
manageable 85° on the warmest of summer days—I'd started
feeling so bad that Moe was all alone. I didn't want us tripping
over her at the new digs, but I couldn't bear to think about
her alone all day, so I'd fetch her up when I could and let her
ride along for deliveries.

Dogs love car rides and Moe was no exception, wind in
her hair, tongue off to the side flapping in the breeze, all that
jazz. That didn't last but a month or so. I caught her eating a
cake one afternoon after getting held up chitchatting on a
delivery. She'd opened the box with what had to be an
impressive nuzzling technique and the cake was wrecked.
This set me back, and I did not have time to remake cakes
with dog bites in them. "Sorry, Moe." She was off deliveries
for life.

o o o

That fall, Helen went into labor without even realizing it was
happening. Talk about being devoted to the job.

She was on Piedmont Road, about a mile out, getting
office supplies when, in her words, "I up and wet my pants."
That's how she remembered it, anyway. Then, she told me
she'd said to the gal Xeroxing that it was the second time that
day where her bladder had let loose.

"It just keeps letting loose. Can you believe that
nonsense?"

"Huh?" was the Xerox gal's reaction.

Then, when Helen got back to Howell Mill, she told me about her runaway bladder, which rendered a different reaction.

"Your water broke! Oh, my God, when did it start? This morning? That's ages ago!"

And off to the hospital we went, Helen and I, a couple of platonic life partners. Did we even call Dave? I cannot remember.

At the hospital, it was all these extremely pregnant women with their husbands, and us. Back in 1987 Atlanta, things were pretty straightforward in the waiting room of a maternity ward. Lordy, did we throw off the feng shui in there.

"Who's with Helen Cleveland?" a nurse came out and asked shortly after scooping her up.

I jumped up and announced, "I am! I am!" in front of all the dads.

Fortunately, Dave arrived before she gave birth, and I went back to work.

o o o

Gamble, Helen and Dave's first child, had arrived a month early.

She had left me high and dry, not so much as a goodbye, the new baby and his round-the-clock demands trumping Piece of Cake and her perpetual needs.

With us pulling the weight of a dozen employees, Helen's midday, middle-of-the-work-week birth had me out six helpers. That's twelve hands!

I had my first real nervous cakedown. I'd openly cry, then crack eggs. Cry, then crack eggs. Cry, then crack eggs. Then, I'd go wash dishes for a couple hours to cool down (on the inside). I was always happy and willing to do anything, as I'd never ask someone to do something I didn't want to do. Maybe washing dishes was meditative, too, no reading or watching the clock required.

Because we weren't letting anyone bake the cakes, mama bear nightmares that we were, I felt alone on POC Island. Terrified comes to mind. And I was too busy making cakes—dozens a day now—to hire more people to help make cakes. Or give me therapy, talk me off the batter-encrusted precipice we'd created. Yank me back from that lonely, ominous edge that seemed to be rising like bread in an oven as I was sinking. It felt like I was being swallowed in the fashion a boa eats its prey, slow and steady. That figurative pain, the impending doom, had me all kinds of panicked.

*What happens if I can't keep up???*

Not once in my life had that ever happened. I have always kept up. I'm a card carrying on-timer. And when I set a goal, I reach it. It's what I've been trained to do. My parents didn't even believe in a Plan B. We never talked about managing failure.

By high school, I was alone with them, as Robb and Belinda were off to college. During dinnertime, which was our time to regroup and discuss everyone's plans over cardboard chicken and steamed spinach (they were always on some crazy diet by then), the possibility of failure was never addressed. Not meeting goals and obligations was like not putting on pants before you left the house for the day: it wasn't an option.

So, there was that. I wasn't allowed to fail. But I honestly didn't even know how to hire people, not for real. I still found time for social gatherings, the place where we'd found all our employees to date. So, even though it wasn't my plan, I had that to fall back on, except there was no time for that. I didn't know what to do beyond cry and crack eggs.

If you're wondering what my idea of a social gathering is, it could be an office Christmas party at Stooge's or two or more people who start chatting in line at the bagel shop. (We still ate carbs for breakfast in the early '90s.) In Atlanta, a trip to the grocery store or run through a park could turn into a social gathering. I would go on to meet future employees at these various, offbeat gatherings, such as spin class, an art show my mom organized, Belinda's third baby shower, and the list goes on.

The point is we never thought anything through. Helen was pregnant for eight whole months and it never occurred to us to have a single conversation about the shift that would occur once the baby was living on the outside.

IF YOU'RE WORKING WITH A PREGNANT PERSON…
THEY WILL EVENTUALLY GIVE BIRTH

This wasn't another Oven Rack Epiphany, but it shot to the top of our Cake-isms like nobody's business. And it was already October...and we all knew what that meant.

o o o

By Christmas, my mom had become one of my regular delivery people. Not that Helen wasn't back at it. I remember coming in at the crack of dawn as she was heading out to deliver cakes, a sleeping baby Gamble strapped safely in the car seat, boxed and bowed cakes piled on either side of him. She had a brand-new baby and was driving around delivering cakes. (Helen was awarded Most Cake-ish that month.) We still hadn't hired more permanent employees. Absurd is a word that comes to mind.

We'd brought in more temps earlier in the season that year to give Helen a couple of weeks of maternity leave (and by a couple, I mean two). Did you know that, in Estonia,[3] employees get eighty-five weeks of maternity leave with full pay? In Japan, it's a year, and the dads get time off, too—with pay. I wonder how Susumu kept his pizza joint going when one of his helping hands got pregnant and showed up for work a year later, ready to rock and roll. Talk about stress.

College kids. They saved us. Jennifer was back with a sister or two and they had friends. Cute friends who were boys. These cute boys were on winter break, and they brought in more cute girls who were on winter break. We'd rallied

---

[3] I have no idea where it is, either.

twenty or so of them. They'd weave in and out of POC at their own convenience, washing dishes, putting bows on boxes, and driving, driving, driving cakes all over Atlanta, spreading the POC holiday cheer.

"You've got *who* delivering *what?*" Robb was all over me.

"Some nice college kids."

"They come in *when?* Whenever they want? How many?"

"Well, I don't want to pressure them while they're on break."

"You don't know how many employees you have? Or when they show up?"

"Yes. Or, no. What was the question?"

Robb was really incensed. "What did you do, bop into a house on fraternity row and ask the boys if they felt like making some money this holiday season?"

"No, but that's a great idea for next year."

"Have you bothered to verify anyone? Get their social security number for tax purposes? Check their driver's license? Confirm they can all legally drive and aren't criminals?"

This was why I didn't go into law.

"Melissa, do you understand the kind of trouble you could be in if something went wrong?"

I understood the kind of panic I'd continue to endure if our cakes weren't delivered on time, and I couldn't think beyond that. (I had just recovered from another nervous cakedown.)

Robb knew it was useless to reason with me. He'd been trying to reason with me for almost thirty years by that point, so he knew the futility of it better than anyone.

I needed drivers any way I could get them. College kids had the time and the energy to help. They wanted extra money and they didn't squabble over their hourly rate, as they were thrilled to be making their own hours and adding to their beer fund. And, they didn't sweat about getting lost all over Atlanta. They actually seemed to be adept at reading maps. There was no GPS, no WAZE. We had atlases of Atlanta and foldup maps from the 7-Eleven. Those were our guides.

The college kids were chill but effective.

They always worked out fine.

Surviving holiday #3 at the new POC location. ✔

After making it through one whole year, including our first holiday season outside my pint-sized condo, I realized I had experienced a lot of relief in the sense that there weren't people traipsing all over my apartment. It made the business feel more authentic, too.

We were on course.

# 14

## OUR BIG FISH WANTS A BIG POND

Little did we realize how the business would grow once we had a location to accommodate her expansion. We'd hit the jackpot at Howell Mill in this regard. We'd taken the goldfish out of the bowl and put her into the koi pond and, boy, did she adapt...swimmingly.

We shared a wall with a man who grew plants for offices. I forgot to mention him earlier, but he outgrew that space by year two, so we took it over. Then, our repair guy Carl Chin moved out and we took over his space shortly thereafter. Then Helen's sister, Margaret, left and we nabbed her space. And on and on it went. Eight hundred square feet turned into 1,600, then 2,400, and the koi pond turned lake *turned Great Lake* by year three at Howell Mill, and POC just kept expanding to fit her new environment.

In June of 1988, when the business slowed just enough to make life manageable, and schools were let out for the year, we made time for more social gatherings. Finally. "Thank you, summertime." This resulted in staff.

Were we still terrified no one could make the cake batter with the same kind of overly tired, adrenaline-charged, manic enthusiasm we could? Yes, yes, we were. But it was time to let go.

Payroll.

So, we established that, a thing called "payroll." I had been handwriting checks to Melinda and Jen and her sisters and our other holiday crew and had no organization about it beyond carbon copies tucked inside ledgers housed in drawers. I needed a bookkeeper. Writing checks and withholding taxes was cumbersome to do manually and I was always doing it on the fly, which added mega stress to the mix. I wasn't a CPA. I had to hire a pro. It was much easier letting go of the books over the baked goods, thank goodness. We have the same lifesaving accountant to this day. (Thanks, Shawn.)

Establishing a framework of structure in a business that was thriving on sweat equity, knock-knock jokes, and Georgia sunshine was like asking me to start wearing a scuba suit to work. It was all kinds of uncomfortable. *I don't care how good Nancy looks in her white chef's coat.* Everything about business ownership had been so random up to that point, and we'd found comfort in that. There was something intangible and magical about it, like Piece of Cake was a living, breathing organism responsible for her own well-being as much as we were. It wouldn't be until we moved to Collier Road in 2013, that I would be able to look back and understand how crazy it was, staying afloat and growing without a plan and living up to all our obligations at all costs.

The mechanics of the business, being a half-step behind the growth, fueled our commitment. We paid for everything like a mob boss: in cold, hard cash, which was good for the company—but was it worth the price of recurring mental collapse? That answer was edging ever closer toward probably not.

Sanity aside, regular staff made sense in that we were always so welcoming of every kind of character. We've both always found people to be downright entertaining, relishing anything from light banter to deep conversations with friends and strangers alike. We were social butterflies, flitting around and fitting in everywhere. "Tell us about your favorite book. Your worst date. Your most embarrassing moment." We were all ears and opinions whether you wanted them or not but did not want to be your superiors, however. If we could get past the image of what the world thought a boss looked like and create our own version *from scratch,* maybe then we could escort "her highness" into a bright-looking future. It was, after all, what she was telling us to do....

## IF CHANGE FINDS YOU, LEAP INTO HER ARMS

# 15

## WHITE LUNG SPRAY

Some of our initial 1989 hires included Donna, Natalie, Harriet, Elizabeth, Saretta, Louise 1, Louise 2, Louise 3, and a man named Page. These fine folks became known as the Cakers.

Birth names didn't last long at POC. They soon went by Mrs. Wiggins, Fuzz, Stare-A, John with the Rolex, Weazer 1, 2, and 3, and Mr. Griffey.

Mrs. Wiggins became famous for filing her nails while the phone rang off the hook beside her. Sometimes, when answered, she'd stretch phone orders out as long as possible to avoid having to take another call. We really weren't customer centric. Thank goodness no one could find us.

Mr. Griffey was an MBA who would never bring lunch to work because of a special program he called Mooch-a-Meal.

Weazer 2's husband would frequently call her with an emergency. "Come home right now. I think you left the faucet on!" This generally meant her baby's diaper needed changing. She always came back to work (if you could call it work). Our staff consisted of a bunch of attractive, articulate, well-educated young people with a natural proclivity for hard work and good gossip.

Say you were between jobs or going through a divorce or having some problems adjusting to your new medication or just needed a nice place to go every day—you'd be an ideal candidate for employment at Piece of Cake. There were no formal interviews. If you turned up with a resume, we would double over and go into the Nancy-with-the-coat story. Occasionally, to put a new hire at ease, I'd suggest they "come on in and work here for a while, just to see how it goes."

Making the leap to hire people to take over the cake baking was huge. We needed cakes around the clock but there was no way I was going to tell people when to arrive, when to go home, or how often to show up. Who does that?

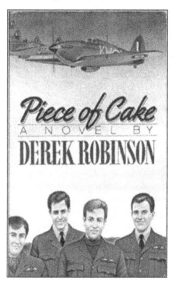

And it was very unlikely that anyone was getting any training. Beyond enforcing the importance of following the recipes, Helen and I didn't train anyone. We did have an employee manual. God knows when it turned up or who'd left it, but it was a from boys-to-men action, thriller, romance novel wryly titled *Piece of Cake.* If asked, we'd direct newcomers to that for a giggle.

It didn't take anyone too long to realize that, at POC, you either found your way or you didn't.

Conversely, just as we never perused a resume, had anyone endure a formal interview, looked at a driver's license, or checked your credit score before hiring, you didn't have to worry about being fired, either. Only one or two people in the history of the company, over thirty-five years, have ever been terminated. And one of them showed up for work the next day, anyway.

If you weren't a good fit, you'd figure it out. You might notice you weren't quite included in the general mayhem, and, then, eventually, you would just drift off to something else, to somewhere else. Your special superpowers, whatever those were, prevented you from being sucked into the POC vortex. Like radiation on the outskirts of a black hole, you were comprised of particles that tunneled you out prior to total annihilation. Good for you! We wished you well.

Some left more suddenly, of course. Once, a woman went out for lunch on her first day and never came back. That was a clean break.

We had needed Cakers ASAP. So, once those roles were filled, there was an unwritten system in place by year's end, a hierarchy if you will.

A typical starting point to your career at Piece of Cake might be slopping batter into cake pans. Mrs. Wiggins (the witty blonde who was known to the outside world as Donna), said she did that all day, every day, for the first several weeks of her tenure. Then, you might graduate to spraying the pans with an oil-based aerosol we referred to as White Lung Spray.

Perhaps, you'd be on dish washing detail, which was safer than inhaling White Lung Spray[4] all day but not quite as fun. You couldn't hear all the drama with the water running and the pans clanking. If you graduated from those tasks, and only you could endow yourself with a "diploma," you were allowed to start mixing the batter, watching the cakes bake, and frosting them. If you got all that down and you wanted to spread your wings—assuming you were particularly skilled at turning a witty phrase or were a solid source for prime gossip—you could nab a seat at the wrapping table.

This was where the cakes were packed into white boxes and tied with a beautiful ribbon that was hand curled to perfection. So, I guess you had to possess that talent, too.

The next position, however strange in the lineup, was delivering. It wasn't that people vied for this gig. I think it was last in line actually, because it was important to learn about *and gain respect for* the caking and baking and boxing part of the business before venturing outside the walls of The Ward. Yes, by this point, POC herself had a special nickname, too.

So, even though we developed a fairly egalitarian society, there was some framework of hierarchy that was not ignored. Not to mention our greatest divide, that of the Carpets and the Tiles, or as we called it: *Carpets v. Tiles.* This should be self-explanatory, as everything about POC is but, to be clear: the Carpets worked in the carpeted area where they took orders and where the finished cakes would arrive for boxing,

---

[4] We have not used this aerosol since the early nineties.

bowing, and delivery. The Tiles were in the back mixing, baking, and dishwashing.

Did the job of the Carpets require less physical labor? Sure. Did they go home less sweaty and with cleaner clothes? Yup. Well, then, why would anybody wanna be a Tile? Because the Carpets had to manage the Customer. (Take a minute to think about that.)

*One Mississippi....*

The Carpets answered phones, took orders, shipped the cakes, and, occasionally, they had to pay attention to any customers who insisted on showing up in person. So, they needed to be born with a natural level of tolerance for other people, as that quality cannot be taught.

o o o

In the new Buckhead shop, things are a little more customer friendly these days. There's a counter you can walk right up to, several attentive employees waiting to serve you, and enticing retail items to browse through if you're kept waiting a few moments. But, in the old location, the famous Howell Mill basement, a customer showing up elicited the same reaction as flicking on the lights in a dark kitchen on a humid summer night. Everyone scattered like roaches.

Page (*aka* Mr. Griffey) recalls that when we made the move to Buckhead, the staff had hoped for some sort of "construction solution" to keep customers away. I was all about accommodating my employees.

"Maybe you could build a wall that could keep them out of the store altogether, so they wouldn't interfere with our work?" I begged the question to our architect.

He replied, "We can't do it. We have to follow code after all, Miss Melissa. People have to be able to enter and exit per code, which includes being able to see the entrance and exit. You understand."

Sadly, I did.

# 16

## BEHIND THE MAGIC CURTAIN

The Ward had what we called the Mr. Ed door. It was a Dutch door with the top half always kept in the **OPEN** position, so the Carpets could see any customers who felt the need to arrive to the store in person. The problem was the Carpets couldn't see them entering because of the position of their desks and the wrapping tables, so they'd have to wait until somebody over in the Tiles noticed a customer pacing around to give them a shout-out.

Mrs. Wiggins, who was in charge of customer care, couldn't see the walk-ins, either. Between the poor angle of her desk, and the phoned-in orders she'd get so wrapped up in, the rest of the world would cease to exist. She'd been gifted with one of those 1-900-number phone voices. That was her first problem. And, two, Mrs. Wiggins found anything fascinating. You could tell her you were pregnant with your first child or you'd just finished brushing your teeth and you'd get the same reaction: *"Oh my goodness, congratulations. Tell me all about it! And start at the beginning. Did you plan it?"* Mr. Griffey handled ten orders in the time she'd spend taking one. But, oh the dirt she'd acquire whilst on those calls.

Beyond the Mr. Ed door, a dog was generally barking, babies would be cruising around in their walkers giggling (or having a finger-full of frosting stuffed in their mouths to keep 'em content if they weren't), and we'd all be elbow-high in eggshells, cake batter, and the latest dirt. It was plain hard to notice when customers came in. There was just too much commotion.

Not to say we didn't love customers. But we wouldn't have official storefront until 1996 at our Buckhead location, the year Atlanta hosted the Olympics. And, boy, were we busy then.

Anyway, people just started dropping by to pick up their cakes one day, even though we were going to deliver them. We never told them to, and we certainly never wanted them to. It was always a madhouse, and we wanted to remain mysterious like the Great Oz. That might have been our only goal come to think of it. The business was supposed to be 100 percent delivery. The *Wall Street Journal* had said delivery was the next big thing, and I had abided. There was no reason to come inside, except that the buzz inside The Ward was kinetic, frenetic, chaotic, contagious, and wrapped in ribbons of belly laughs and joy. They wanted to see what was behind the damn curtain.

Like most things at POC, customers coming in to pick up their cakes evolved organically. So, when it started happening, we surely weren't going to put a halt to it. Once people started hanging out at the Mr. Ed door, waiting, staring at all of us baking cakes, which was just plain awkward, we knew it was time for change. So, we shoved a few brand-new candles that were lying around the store on Mr. Ed's frame and called it a pickup window. Customers started studying them instead of us. "Are these...for sale? This one smells amazing."

When we would finally move to Buckhead, despite my POC family vying for a "wall," I realized there could be more potential if we built a pickup window of sorts instead.

○ ○ ○

Nowadays, at Collier Road, the cake "pickup area" resembles a full-blown gift shop. We make regular trips to Atlanta's wholesale Gift Mart to find the latest must-have chachkis, from teapots to children's gifts to other food items like our gluten-free chocolate cupcakes, which we've sold for almost a decade now.

As usual, we don't set any sort of budget for what we spend on retail. We just buy what we like and most of it ends up selling.

# 17

## "STICK 'EM UP, MISS MELISSA!"

Despite the fact that we were still technically *delivery only*, Piece of Cake has been the target of more than one robbery.

Helen had just had her second baby, it was 1990, and she was back in the Dairy nursing Kent. Gamble, her toddler, was hanging around up front. I was sitting at my desk. A couple of Cakers were hanging out with me, waiting for quitting time, which was four thirty.

That's when this man with a broken-off liquor bottle in one hand and a paper bag over his head—with not two eye holes but an entire circle cut out of the middle, so you could pretty much see his whole face—walked in.

Everybody just sort of froze, stunned in place.

Well, before he had time to say, "Stick 'em up!" I yelled from behind my desk, "Ronald, what are you doing?" (Note: I've changed his name to protect the guilty.)

I was fairly certain it was my mother's housekeeper's boyfriend. But then I thought: *Maybe it's an Eastern Onion, a stripper that just looks like Ronald.*

Anyway, everyone took off, splaying out in all directions, and no one grabbed Gamble. And someone, I can't remember who, ran next door and called 911, while two others ran up to the gas station at the top of the hill. Meanwhile, Helen was still back in the Dairy nursing, oblivious to the whole thing.

So, I was left standing there by my desk area because everyone else had taken off and I couldn't get out. I had one eye on Gamble, but he seemed to be of no interest to Ronald, so that was a relief. I wasn't even sure Ronald could see him, as he had limited-to-no peripheral vision with that bag on his head.

So, Ronald boxed me in a corner, and we stood there like a Mexican standoff. Finally, I didn't know what else to do so I kicked him where you're supposed to.

At that, he came flying over the desk into the open drawer where the money was. I should've been terrified. The man was twice my size and had a deadly weapon. But I couldn't get past the fact that he'd botched the whole bit with the mask. It was hilarious.

Anyway, he got the bag of money—and just after I had done the whole Visa thing, too, where you have to call it all in, which is a major production. So, I tried to negotiate with him. "Just take a little cash, Ronald, if you want to. Leave all the paperwork. I just finished that!"

He ran out with the whole damn bag.

That's when I ran right after him.

He ran up the hill toward the gas station.

I ran up the hill toward the gas station.

We got there to discover my two Cakers were just hanging out. "Go!" I yelled, and they started chasing him, too.

This off-duty cop happened to drive by, and I guess he thought it looked like something was up—all these women chasing this one man with a brown bag over his head and a big bag of money in his hand. So, the cop caught up, parked, jumped out, and pinned Ronald to the ground in no time.

And that was that.

We all hovered as the police officer cuffed him and read him his rights.

He was not an Eastern Onion strip-o-gram but my mother's housekeeper's boyfriend for sure. "Miss Melissa, help me!" he kept saying as he was getting cuffed. "You gotta help me get out of this!"

About six months later, I started receiving letters from prison with apology after apology.

*Dear Miss Melissa,*
*It was the vodka that made me do it....*
*Ronald*

*Dear Miss Melissa,*
*I am so sorry about robbing you. I've always liked you.*
*Please don't take it personally.*
*Ronald*

*Dear Miss Melissa,*

*The more I've thought about why I did what I did, it's because you've always been so nice to me. So, thank you for that, Miss Melissa, and I apologize for my wrongdoing.*

*Ronald*

DON'T LEAVE BABIES OR BAGS OF MONEY UNATTENDED

# 18

## THE BOMB

Nowadays, we have a courier service. But, back in the olden days, if you graduated to deliveries, you jumped in something we called The Bomb, a dismal heap of unknown make and model. Who knows where we got it, possibly also at the Goodwill. *Or maybe it was lying on the side of the road near the Goodwill?*

After packing The Bomb with a dozen cakes in the back, a dozen in the trunk, and another half dozen riding shotgun, you'd head out for parts unknown and hopefully return cake-free with your wits about you. This worked for some time.

But, as the business grew, and we quadrupled in size and added a customer service pickup window, we thought it might be nice to advertise while we were out on deliveries. We tried attaching a plastic box-like contraption to the top of the automobile—a big, bright, white cake box complete with a red bow. Our logo had come to life in 3D form. This was ingenious and innovative, and worked well to identify us.

But the 1990s weren't ready for this kind of advertising. We might as well have been cruising around town and taking corners on two wheels.

People started calling in like crazy, tattling on our delivery team.

*"I think I saw one of your cars driving up over curbs and backing into a telephone pole downtown on Peachtree."*

*"Your cake car was heading the wrong way down a one-way. I nearly hit a tree!"*

*"I'm pretty sure I saw your car swerving down Piedmont. I think your driver mighta been drinking right there in the car."*

*"Your cake bus ran a red light."*

*"Your delivery car picked up a hitchhiker."*

*"Your cake car was parked outside my nail salon. It's 85° today. Cakes must be melting all over!"*

*"I think I just saw my daughter driving around in that god-awful cake bus of yours. Can you give her another task? She can't be seen in that vehicle—she's still single."*

Any one of those scenarios could have been an accurate appraisal of the goings on during deliveries. We had to ixnay the cake box. We were too exposed.

But, The Bomb was a staple, and she would continue to live out her life as part of the POC team for years to come. No matter how she begged—she needed an alignment, a new muffler, tires, brakes, and don't get me started on the paint job—we refused to put her down. By the time we did, she looked much like the car from *Planes, Trains and Automobiles.* No joke (well, maybe a little).

I remember telling my POCsters to say goodbye to The Bomb one day. I was taking her to her grave (Cash for Clunkers). They laughed and said, "I bet you won't get fifty bucks for that thing!"

Did I show them! I came back with a check for fifty-one.

o o o

In the days before cell phones, smartphones, and GPS, finding the right address in a city with millions of residents could be challenging. And bursting into tears whilst attempting this feat was not uncommon. One day, an employee named Sally stormed in from a day of deliveries and shouted, "You sent me to a crack house! I quit!"

We didn't know what to tell her, as POC did not discriminate. If a crack dealer or crack user wanted a cake, we made them a cake. Also, she couldn't quit, as we'd never established a hiring process. So, basically, that was Sally's last day of deliveries. We "reassigned" her, and she was okay after that.

In case you Millennials can't imagine what being lost to the point of tears feels like, here is a page from a 1990s street map of Downtown Atlanta. I'm sweating just looking at it. (And there was no "zoom in" feature.)

Page had the city broken down into delivery zones, which helped. And everyone had their favorite, which helped, too, as they got to know that zone well. Page preferred the downtown route—weaving through the skyscrapers—because the addresses were all so close together. For the really far-out deliveries, places like Lawrenceville and other distant destinations beyond Atlanta's perimeter, there was Pam. Pam used her own set of wheels—a white van—and was happy to drive anywhere. Pam said driving relaxed her. Hence, any location outside the city limits was, and still is, referred to as Pamland.

Some drivers really did stop at the gym or go get their nails done mid-delivery. This was *no bueno*. But, unless someone tattled or performed a citizen's arrest, any excuse they came up with on return worked for us. How could we know how traffic was that day or if they got held up chatting with a customer? We were busy cracking eggs and slinging batter.

The self-enforced system of governing at Howell Mill was working.

Our staff wasn't getting rich, but they weren't suffering through the dullness of entry-level positions at banks or other major corporations, either. "*That's twenty, forty, sixty, eighty— one, and twenty, forty, sixty, eighty—two.*" They were having a blast, making their own hours, and self-delegating tasks. A key element to Piece of Cake's success in the first five years was autonomy. Everyone had the opportunity to claim as much power as they wanted. And, if they did choose to leave, we were a great reference, especially because people created their own job titles.

"*You're calling about Beverly, our Senior Director of Caking? Oh, yes, Beverly was the best Caking Director a company could ask for.*"

"*Steve, our Ingredients Engineer? You can't beat him. Top-notch Ingredients Engineers don't grow on trees, you know....*"

## AUTONOMY IS ITS OWN REWARD

From how many of which cakes to bake to whether we stay open or closed on a certain holiday, employees make those major decisions to this day. But, in the early days, back when Helen and I wouldn't let anyone near our three coveted recipes, we were comfortable with our employees calling all the other shots, too.

Peter, whose previous position was with Merrill Lynch, came aboard the POC crazy train around this time. He'd stay behind to mop daily because he wanted the extra hours. All alone mopping to the sound of silence, he'd notice customers were dropping by after 4:30, knocking on the door, peeking in the windows. Peter concluded there was business to be had by staying open later. And that was that. He reopened the business for another thirty minutes.

Today, closing time is seven o'clock.

Perhaps that's how you inspire long years of loyalty from a staff smart enough to work just about anywhere they want. You allow them the freedom to choose, you trust them blindly, you value their opinion. (And bottomless pitchers of margaritas from US Bar y Grill didn't hurt, either!) A job at Piece of Cake is hard work, often dirty work, and work that pays less than what you might make if you were pursuing the sorts of careers your parents had envisioned. But our employees have always had such a damn good time running the place. We couldn't get in the way of that. Many tell me to this day that working for POC was the best job they ever had.

And in the working world, that is far harder to come by than a corner office with an ocean view.

o o o

By 1996, Piece of Cake headquarters was housed in a sunlight-filled, ivory-colored brick cottage in the heart of Buckhead, one of Atlanta's original exclusive neighborhoods. A century ago, wealthy Atlantans built their mansions along these tree-lined streets north of downtown. The 30305 zip code is one of the prime residential and commercial locations in the city, and among the most affluent in the nation.

Piece of Cake is as much a part of the culture in this neighborhood as any business on Peachtree Street.

# 19

## A WORK-FREE DRUG PLACE

By those in the know, the shop on Howell Mill was commonly referred to as The Ward, but it boasted some other monikers, too: the Work-Free Drug Place, the Home for Wayward Souls, the Black Hole, and the Pokey (the phonetic derivation of the acronym for Piece of Cake, Inc.) were among the others. And, by 1991, there was some evidence to support the notion that it was indeed a haven for substance abusers, criminals, and the mentally imbalanced. Someone had hung *The Doctor Is In* Peanuts poster plainly on my wall. Though not a medical degree from Harvard, "Psychiatric Help 5¢" did add to our credibility.

There was Brent, a sweet artist who wore a vial of lithium around his neck at all times. One Friday, he asked us to lock him inside the store all weekend with some canvases. He said the place inspired him like no other. When we came back on Monday, you should have seen his paintings! (I'm talking about a real artist, whose work sells. The energy inside POC fueled him.)

Drake, the recovering alcoholic—love him to this day!—
had been referred to us by another graduate of a rehab center
in Arizona. Drake loved doing deliveries, as "driving is a
privilege, Miss Melissa." We nonaddicts sometimes forget
that.

Donna kept *The Pill Book* on her desk to keep up with
all her various medications. She and I would get in these
verbal sparring matches early in the workday, then she'd
"manage" her mood and we'd be splitting a sandwich for
lunch. God, how I loved her. She dated this boy who'd bring
her the most magnificent croissants and danishes and the
woman was the size of my pinky finger. Damn, was that
annoying.

And then there was Harriet (Harry) and Louise (Weazer
2). Harry was a full-timer who was younger than all of us, at
just twenty-one. She always had *so* much drama in her life. It
was a daily reminder not to miss our early twenties. Weazer 2
was a few years older and fighting with her boyfriend was a
way of life. Her roommate, Angela, who worked at the Pokey,
too, would come in and say, "Louise was cooking all weekend
again." That was code for fighting with her boyfriend. We
diagnosed another employee, Zoe (Zombie), by armchair
psychology as a manic depressive, paranoid schizophrenic,
and sociopath. We encouraged her to stay around as long as
she wanted to (for obvious reasons).

Our Work-Free Drug Place was also the kind of
establishment where you could find a baby or two wandering
around most days. It had started with Helen's babies and grew

from there. Soon, other women started having babies and they brought them in, too. This happens with a staff of 99 percent women in their late twenties to late thirties. It's an actual job hazard for employers in this line of work, unless you find a work around like we did. (Bakery owners: you have been warned.) This was why we'd devoted a whole storage room to these fine women. "The Dairy," as mentioned in our robbery story, is where they would all go to breastfeed the babies.

It seemed as if I were the only woman who wasn't pregnant or nursing in our employment. Someone asked me in an interview once how I thought all these babies affected business. I responded, "*A baby's no worse than a smoker. We're happy to have people at work. And we're ready to accommodate whatever they have to do.*"

No kidding. It's in writing. Oh, lordy, non-mom that I was, that's what I said.

o o o

Some employees responded better to the stress levels than others. A few were models of efficiency. Others, saddled with their own special quirks, seemed to slow down the process. There was one guy—when Angela got plain sick of stirring and graduated to recipes—who became recognized as our new frosting expert. But he was not known for his speed. On one sunny but tense summer day the beginning of July, I recall asking him to make up another batch of frosting within the hour. We were out, cakes were bare, and customers were on their way in.

An hour later, it was:

—Frosting: 0

—Customers Standing Around Waiting for Frosted Cakes: 5

I went back into the kitchen. "Chris, you are driving me crazy."

"Well," Chris drawled, "you're driving me crazy, too."

Words to live by.

We had our own homeless person: Stinkyman Joe. He'd quote French poetry in exchange for odd jobs and money. We weren't exactly all stocked up on French poetry, but we didn't feel incomplete without it, either. Even so, when Page would tell him we didn't have any work for him that day, he would grab the broom anyway and break into iambic pentameter. And we would pay up.

Occasionally, he'd take his entrepreneurship even further. One day, he pulled a bunch of reject cakes out of the dumpster and set up shop on the corner of Howell Mill and Collier Road. "Piece of Cake cakes!" he yelled. "Fifty bucks!"

Piece of Cake was charging $23 a cake at the time. He wasn't the smartest of salesmen.

Occasionally, someone would actually get hauled away to Peachford, one of the nicest mental hospitals in the area, and the country. But, most days, we would all just hang out together baking cakes. We were the "Original Battered Women." *Am I allowed to say that in this century?*

I couldn't imagine turning someone away for mental health reasons. "*Many hands make light work.*" That's a phrase Grandma Ruth Alice used to say. I was always so grateful that people showed up for work at all. Bring your problems! We can work through them while we're beating batter and frosting cakes.

Wax on.

Then, suddenly, I became one of the crazies.

# 20

## CRY AND CRACK EGGS

You know how some people just aren't lucky in love? Helen wasn't lucky in the au pair department. After she'd lost her sixth hire (*to love, ironically*), she saw it as a sign, but she wanted another child and to watch her kids grow up—and not from the rearview window of The Bomb, as she'd been doing for the better part of four years. So, one day in the winter of '91, Helen asked me to buy her out of the company.

I was devastated.

Yes, the company was thriving, cruising full speed ahead, controlled chaos fueling it like solar panels on a skyrise in the Tropics. I had no complaints. Life was but a dream. But, in that dream I had a business partner. I never wanted to go it alone.

Today, one in five firms with over one million dollars in annual revenue is owned by a woman. That still puts me in the minority, even though America is one of the most liberal countries in the world. (And, according to PayScale, we make $0.81 for every dollar a man makes.) But, back then, in the early nineties, women didn't own big businesses. We ran shops. They were cute. Quaint. Unobtrusive. They were nestled quietly between Chuck's Gun & Pawn and Atlanta Books in an up-and-coming, but-not-quite-there-yet neighborhood in Buckhead.

I didn't want to be standing on the POC mountaintop alone. We'd built the company without a permit in my pint-sized condo kitchen. What if something were to go wrong here, something we'd never thought about? Or, worse. What if something were to go right? Like, really right? Who would help me then?

We had done a local radio interview a few months before she'd dropped this bomb, and you should have seen me. It was divine intervention that it was radio. The listeners couldn't see me sweat and watch as I choked on my words after being asked the simple question: "*What made you start a cake delivery company?*" Helen took over, and I dubbed her the Voice of the Company after that. She couldn't leave.

It was unimaginable to me that Helen wanted to change course. It's not that it didn't make sense, as she had her family to consider, but POC was our other family. We had Movie Mondays, we went to US Bar y Grill for happy hour on Fridays, and we took weekend breaks lakeside—together.

I became paralyzed with fear (but in a get-out-of-bed-before-dawn-and-go-to-work kind of way, naturally). At least, I was able to focus on logistics. That was easier than managing the emotional insecurity I was feeling. We went to a broker who gave us a range for what POC was worth. At the end of the day, he informed us, "It's about what one person is willing to pay and the other is willing to accept." Like in real estate, it was about market value versus appraisal. Agreeing on a figure wasn't the hard part. It wasted time, though, so that was nice.

I tried to imagine the upside of Helen leaving, which would be a pay raise. Her meager wages would be going to me. I'd be making $10 an hour! I'm kidding, of course, but we were still tight with cashflow, and I was trying to calm my nerves about bossing it alone by any means possible. I couldn't imagine, however, that doubling my pay would cut the stress of running the business alone in half. That would have been helpful, but the cakes were still calling, and all I could compute was that I'd now have twice as many cakes to make with half as many hands.

Cry and crack eggs. Cry and crack eggs. Wince, repeat. Overnight, that was my new life. Well, not exactly. I dragged out Helen's exodus over the course of six months, insisting we meet regularly for breakfast at the Okay Café to go over the details. That was really just me clinging to what I thought was a good thing, fearing the one thing, *the only thing*, we can all count on in this world: change. Life is transient. I couldn't believe I was pushing so hard up against something so much bigger than me.

Once word spread about her departure, the voices inside my head were suddenly living on the outside and coming at me from all directions.

*"You need to find a man to help you run this company. That's what you need to do, Melissa."*

*"A man will give you credibility."*

*"You can't run this by yourself, dear."*

*"Does your father have a friend that you could partner with? Your brother?"*

That was the consensus. I needed a new partner and they needed to be a "he."

But why?

Because that was the norm? Because it was safe? Traditional? Did people think that, as a woman, I wasn't capable of taking this company further?

*"If you want to be taken seriously, if you want credibility, you need to find a partner, and it needs to be a man."*

There was my answer.

No, people did not seem to have confidence in me flying solo. The stress of being abandoned was worse than baking 100 cakes in my condo back before I knew how to screw the lightbulb into the lamp and plug it into the outlet.

I would end up joining a "women in business" group, and it was there that I learned most female entrepreneurs split their time between personas to survive. They'd wear a ball-busting work mask while running the company, and save their sweet, laid-back, Southern side for family and friends in their off-time. My one and only persona was more in line with the latter. Because of that, I couldn't even begin to imagine how to force myself into a mold that didn't fit. Maybe that's what made everyone so nervous.

But people wanted to be at Piece of Cake. Employees, customers, family and friends of employees and customers— everybody flocked to the company. We were different. We were where all the action was. POC was a real scene, like Studio 54 in the seventies. And I was the DJ. People would find their groove at POC, their niche. Find their bliss. And as DJ, I had to keep it together, as there was music to be played.

I remembered at some point, on the heels of Helen leaving, thinking that if I heard my name one more time, I was going to leap out a window (yes, a basement window, but still). I had to start parceling out jobs. I couldn't answer to everyone. It was impossible. I couldn't do everything. There weren't enough minutes in an hour.

To put my panic attacks in monetary terms, in 1991, the year I became the sole owner, we'd baked and sold over 20,000 cakes. We were up 63 percent from the year before—I just did the math!—and it was panic central back then at 12,600 cakes. We'd baked and delivered several dozen cakes daily in the off season, and between 600 and 800 cakes (daily) through the holiday season, which was about six weeks long. Yet, we'd only upped our staff by about 6.3 percent since 1990.

But these stats, which proved once again that we (the workers) were one step behind POC, would wind up saving me from a psychotic break ironically.

Now that I was in the boat alone, there was comfort in knowing we were always making money because we were always short on labor because POC was expanding faster than we could keep up. This is not what every company should do, but the constant frenzy of orders coming in and the literal race to deliver them on time gave me the courage to put the notion of having a business partner on the back burner, where it is still simmering to this day, and the good sense to relinquish some of my power to all the dedicated and capable POCsters around me.

## DO NOT UNDERESTIMATE THE POWER OF ORGANIZED CHAOS

With Helen, Piece of Cake was birthed. Over the course of our near-six-year partnership, what looked like an elementary school bake sale out of my condo kitchen multiplied a dozen times over, turning into a formidable enterprise. It wasn't my intention to reach the million-dollar mark in annual revenues—I never had a target—but, by the way we all came together and worked, singularly focused, blinders on before dawn, we plowed ahead toward that finish line and then beyond like thoroughbreds in fear of retirement—or worse!

o o o

Piece of Cake would reach over one million dollars in sales in 1998.

# PART II

# SEMITRAILERS, SEVEN FIGURES, & SATELLITE STORES

"A party without cake is just a meeting."

—Julia Child

# 21

## DELTA SIGMA HIGH

With *The Cake Lady* now flying solo, and the Christmas season around the corner, I needed more employees. That was my focus and thank goodness because, that Christmas, Piece of Cake received its first *really big* order for 600 cakes from a law firm in Tennessee. This meant that one morning during the holidays, we'd be delivering up to 1,200 cakes that we'd baked the night before.

Fifteen cakes had me doing cartwheels in 1985. The following year, 100 cakes blew my mind. Now, it was happening: a law firm a state away wanted 600 cakes.

At all costs, those cakes were getting made. I'd rent a U-Haul to get them delivered if I had to. (I had to!) And I'd drive it myself if it came to that! (It did not, thankfully.)

I had dipped back into my holiday workforce early that season, which had been traditionally filled by the college boys (and sometimes girls) on winter break from University of Georgia in Athens. I told them to bring friends, siblings, girlfriends, ex-girlfriends, anyone with two capable hands and a driver's license. I was still winging it with these kids, using the honor system when writing out paychecks, etc., but most of these freelancers had worked for me during prior seasons, which gave me the security that they were reliable and came with reliable friends, which they did. (The only hiccup would be that I needed them to come to work on time this season and would end up calling their mothers to wake them up most mornings.)

Additionally, if you ran into me while walking Moe or in the bathroom of a bar on a Saturday night, you were interrogated about your tentative holiday engagements and level of interest in a new career path. And, with all that in place, I felt like I had it covered.

The first couple weeks of December went okay....

Then, one night, there was a huge bash at UGA. Keep in mind, Athens is 100 miles away from Atlanta, but these kids lived in the Atlanta area with their parents over break. Well, the next morning, none of our delivery guys made it into work. The place was frantic. I called everyone I knew to help. My mom was out delivering cakes all morning long—*that's the level of desperation of which I'm speaking: Code Mom.*

Finally, late that afternoon, two of my team of twenty boys straggled in extremely hungover and in search of some pot to curb their headaches so they could help out. We phoned "a friend of a friend."

"Well, I'm not really dealing anymore. Are they cute?" the friend-of-a-friend's ex-pot dealer asked.

I assured her they were adorable, to which she responded, "I'm, like, in my bathrobe, but I guess you can send them over anyway."

The two young, adorable, hungover lads set out for her house. One of them came back high but headache-free and was able to lend a hand to the Carpets (no driving for him that evening). The other didn't return to work for five days. He and the friend-of-a-friend's ex-pot dealer would go on to get married.

Along with a welcome shot of testosterone—keep in mind, Page was our only fulltime male employee—our UGA boys also brought a particular element of fun that full-blown, community-dwelling adults simply couldn't.

They had an annual running joke with a plastic cockroach. Every single year, one of the guys would hide it somewhere in the store. This joke was old, and it hardly elicited a rise out of the Carpets or the Tiles, but the college boys couldn't seem to get enough of it and were still in that stage where you laughed at your own jokes, even if no one else did.

Well, the roach joke was retired that Christmas for good when a new kid planted it in a flour bin that Natalie was using to mix batter for blueberry pound cakes. She was talking a blue streak as usual and dipping out flour with a two-cup scoop. Hours later, after the cakes had been baked, wrapped, and sent on their merry holiday way, Joe College asked Natalie why she hadn't bothered to comment on the roach.

"What roach?" Natalie asked.

That quieted the room.

Nobody ever called to complain, thank goodness.

The theory we've accepted is that when the cakes baked, the heat of the oven must have melted the roach enough that it resembled a big hunk of blueberry.

Another one of the Athens guys came complete with a talking toilet seat that he'd plant periodically in the Ladies Room. Whenever anyone sat down, a loud voice would boom, *"Hey, I'm working down here!"* A little juvenile, perhaps, but it added to the scenery in there, as the walls were plastered with quirky newspaper clippings.

"Many Weapons Found in Gun Shop Raid"
"Ten Keys to Getting Grammer Right"
"Forecast Calls for Weather on Thursday"
"Why I'm Hanging onto a Loser"
"Obesity Linked to Overeating"

One Christmas Eve, we ended the night with twenty to thirty extra cakes, just sitting there, waiting to be eaten. It was odd, but there weren't any orders in the "queue," so I bid everyone "happy holidays," as I handed them a cake. With just a few of us left, I noticed some sheets of paper had fallen between the file folder and wall—orders for about thirty cakes, of course. And back to work we went. Recreating the cakes I'd given away.

During another mad holiday hustle, the handle fell off the front door, which locked everybody in. The Ward had been built partially underground with cinder block walls and glass block windows. There was literally NO WAY OUT. We had a customer locked in with us who had just come from signing her divorce papers. She was picking up a cake for this party she was throwing for herself. We felt so badly, we fed her lunch while we waited.

And waited.

And waited.

Meanwhile, Weazer 2 was supposed to go pick up her kid from school. She had to call her husband to go. One of our college kids had come back from making deliveries and she was standing outside, occasionally peeking in through the tiny hole the handle had left—our only view of the outside world, the outside world's only view in—to giggle and gawk. Another employee had just loaded up her car with a bunch of cakes. She was grabbing the last two when she got locked in with us. There was this customer out there trying to get in through a crack in the wall or God knows how. He needed his chocolate cake in a bad way. We finally got him to browse through the cakes in the other delivery car, take a chocolate one, and leave a check.

It was several hours before the locksmith arrived to fix the door. Of course, the show went on. After the chocolate cake guy left, we got smart and posted a Caker in a chair in front of the door handle. She'd yell to all the outside customers to look through the cakes in the car, grab the type they'd ordered, and kindly leave cash or a check.

That's the kind of place it was, someplace where the door handle could just come off in your hand, leaving the staff in some kind of hostage situation, forcing the customers into a grab-and-go system of pickup. "Just grab the one that looks right and go!"

Was Susumu dealing with these sorts of things? Were there boxes of pizzas stacked in clumsy columns in some jacked-up car outside his pizza parlor? Was he staring at them through a peephole in his door because he'd locked himself in? Did these offbeat occurrences happen to every young business owner?

But the connections, from love interests to career contacts, were cultivated round the clock at Piece of Cake. It was known as something of a hub for the community at large. "It's the gossip center of Atlanta," Angela said once, beaming with pride that she was at the nucleus of it all. She was square on. We knew everything. Who was getting married, who was getting divorced, who was pregnant. Who was doing what to whom and when. We'd know the home game and away game high school sports schedules by heart. We were *Melrose Place* meets the *National Inquirer.* Or *Keeping Up With the Kardashians* meets *TMZ* for you under forties.

If someone needed a zip code to a town on the outskirts of Atlanta for, say, a Christmas card or whatever, they'd call us. We were delivering all over by that point.

"That's 30305," I'd say.

"No, I think it's 30338," Fuzz would retort. "Out in Pamland."

We'd spar and then figure it out.

We got calls about deaths or births before the *Atlanta Journal.* Fuzz would answer those. She'd left her day job at Merrill Lynch for Piece of Cake, so the least we could do was put her in charge of time-sensitive information. She gave everyone the skinny on the when and where of funerals, weddings, births, birthdays, etc.

People would even call and say things like, "We're having poached salmon for dinner. What goes with that?" Like we were supposed to know.

Donna would say, "Pinot grigio and carrot cake, of course."

Our word was gold. Salmon and carrot cake it was. *Who knew?*

We did. Even when we didn't know, we knew.

That's when we added "World Headquarters" to POC's list of monikers. And that name went viral long before the word viral would go viral.

# 22

## "THE SWORD OF POWER!"

By '95, ten years since her humble beginnings, there was a real buzz about Piece of Cake. It *was* a home for wayward souls, an in-between kind of place, a Work-Free Drug Place, the Pokey, World Headquarters. It was a one-woman-owned business that had become the center of Atlanta's Universe, and without even trying. And POC had one heck of a product. The cakes were unrivaled in quality, their simplicity somehow making them unique. Our promise to deliver and our customer service, however eccentric, was unparalleled. The foundation had been set, and now I was building the house, one brick at a time.

I've heard new business owners say things like, "For the first few years forget about a social life, your family, your friends. If you're interested in becoming successful, you have to bury yourself in the business." We buried ourselves for sure but welcomed family and friends to spin along with us in our POC vortex. We tied the proverbial apron around their waists and put the willing to work. We paid them just to show up, hoping that our original brand of fun would entice them to come back day after day despite the cake dust lodged in their nostrils. We weren't above bribing or begging. And when we panicked, it showed. We looked genuinely frazzled, so people wanted to help then, too. We weren't above pity, either.

Even when working at POC during the holiday rush scored higher than "divorce" on the Holmes-Rahe Stress Scale, people wanted to be right in the thick of it, spinning at the speed of light alongside us. (The rate of spin at the center of a black hole is just shy of the speed of light, in case you were wondering.)

### Holmes and Rahe Stress Scale

| Life Event | Value |
|---|---|
| Death of a spouse | 100 |
| Working at POC during the holiday rush | 99 |
| Divorce | 73 |
| Marital separation | 65 |
| Jail term | 63 |
| Death of a close family member | 63 |
| Personal injury or illness | 53 |
| Marriage | 50 |
| Fired at work | 47 |
| Marital reconciliation | 45 |
| Retirement | 45 |
| Change in health of family member | 44 |
| Pregnancy | 40 |
| Sex difficulties | 39 |
| Gain of new family member | 39 |
| Business readjustment | 39 |
| Change in financial state | 38 |
| Death of a close friend | 37 |
| Change to a different line of work | 36 |
| Change in number of arguments with spouse | 35 |
| Home mortgage over $100,000 | 31 |

| Life Event | Value |
|---|---|
| Foreclosure or mortgage or loan | 30 |
| Change in responsibilities at work | 29 |
| Son or daughter leaving home | 29 |
| Trouble with in-laws | 29 |
| Outstanding personal achievement | 28 |
| Spouse begins or stops work | 26 |
| Begin or end school | 26 |
| Change in living conditions | 25 |
| Revision of personal habits | 24 |
| Trouble with boss | 23 |
| Change in work hours or conditions | 20 |
| Change in residence | 20 |
| Change in schools | 20 |
| Change in recreation | 19 |
| Change in church activities | 19 |
| Change in social activities | 18 |
| Mortgage or loan of less than $100,000 | 17 |
| Change in sleeping habits | 16 |
| Change in number of family get-togethers | 15 |
| Change in eating habits | 15 |

Some POCsters stayed a year or two. Some stayed for fifteen. Some are still here. Some left and came back.

At a certain point, though, the charm of the Howell Mill location grew thin. It was totally stressful with its Third World working conditions.

The air conditioning didn't work, the plumbing was shot, we had no storage, no parking, no windows to crack for even a smidge of fresh air. Swarms of people—the Carpets, the Tiles, the customers(!)—we were all just on top of each other. We had outgrown the Howell Mill building long before we decided it was time to move on and move up.

In typical Piece of Cake fashion, I didn't want to jump until I was sure the waters were shark free. But I also didn't want anyone else being surprised by predators because I always want to do the right thing. So, ready or not, I went to my landlord to tell him that I was thinking about looking around for a larger, more accommodating space. We'd had a great relationship for a whole decade, and the advanced warning was a courtesy. I emphasized that "I'm just in the 'thinking about it' phase...and Lord knows that could last six, eight, nine months or more!" Then, we laughed, I thanked him for his time, and left feeling good about that deed.

That should have been a sign, as no good deed....

Two days later, Dr. Dinwald came up to me and said, "I've found somebody to rent your space. This is your ninety-day notice."

And that was that.

Thank goodness Belinda's husband, Ken, was in real estate. He found three places that I thought would work, which was shocking, as I'm the pickiest person I know. We'd get on a roll with one and the deal would crumble. Then we'd jump on the next, and that deal would crumble. When all was said and done, the building on Roswell Road was to be our destination because that was the deal that went through.

The new location was right in the heart of Buckhead. It needed a lot of work to become what (for the first time ever) I was envisioning—a sunlight-filled, charming, cottage-like cake shop. We had three months to reconstruct it.

Moving into that building was a major learning curve. The builder and the architect would get into huge fights and I'd be like, "Wait a minute, I think I'm the client here. Don't fight on my time." Anyway, I didn't know the first thing about reconstructing a building, but I learned several valuable lessons, two of which are: Don't pay for things ahead of time. And, plan for delays.

We ended up having to move in before we were finished.

The working conditions were more than comfortable, they were luxurious. I never had an office before, and now I did. An office! *Whatever will I put in it?* Took about four days before you couldn't see the top of my desk.

You should have seen the bathrooms. You know those gas station restrooms they show on TV where people are always getting mugged and murdered? That's what the bathrooms looked like at Howell Mill. Never dawned on me how nice it would be to *not* have to close the door with your elbow, hold your breath while tinkling, and flush with your foot when you're done.

And the layout for the employees? Well, the people dealing with the customers, the Carpets, and the people baking the cakes, the Tiles, were suddenly in two different worlds. This caused a marked cultural shift in the company, creating a vastly more structured workplace without me doing a thing. Howell Mill was really one big room. It was just that half the room was all tables, boxes, and phones, and the other half was all ingredients, mixers, and ovens. Suddenly, there was order in the POC court. The front area was separate from the kitchen. Of course, I still had the issue of staff. Fourteen regular employees keeping six industrial ovens going year-round over at The Ward was not going to cut it here. We were selling over 35,000 cakes annually by this point. The business had grown by almost 200 percent, and the staff by about 20 percent. But my longtimes had really stepped up, like Fuzz, Harriet, Donna, Natalie, Page, and the Louises. The employees that had POC in their bones knew where, when, and how to lend a hand to keep our ship cruising full speed ahead.

Once we got rolling—though it looked like the Property Brothers had transformed us—certain features began to resemble home. For example, my office, which was at the end of a hallway, started serving as a go-between. It separated the baking area from the storefront. I loved the action.

Just blocks away, other bakeries were closing down as we were opening our doors. Two of the employees from one of them, a Hispanic couple, stopped in to inquire about job openings. This couple shined like nobody's business. I hired them on the spot. A couple weeks into their new employment, they mentioned something about a sister in need of work. What a coincidence. I was in need of help! Then, it was a cousin. Then a nephew. Then an aunt. I blinked, and my kitchen staff were all related to each other and speaking Spanish. Except for the two Bosnians I'd picked up somewhere, they were speaking Croatian.

This shift in the workforce changed my role and how I managed the kitchen staff. After years of giving my employees wake-up calls, they arrived on time. After bribing them with margaritas to stay after hours, they worked until the job was complete, and they did it sober. They started arriving before me; meaning, I stopped coming in for the pre-dawn prep entirely. My new staff caught onto the system and took it over. My life became so easy by comparison. Now, I'm not knocking young, single, white people with our young, single, white-people problems. Don't get me wrong. But this was one of those things that made me go "wow," like that White Chocolate Layer Cake from the dingo breeder did the first time I tasted it.

Communication could have been an issue. I didn't speak Spanish and they didn't speak English, not really. But, you sort of show somebody how to do something and then they just do it. I don't think my new staff could read my recipes, per se, but they studied the system and worked it out. To this day, it's always worked out. For insurance issues or vacation time, sometimes a kid will call in to translate for mom or dad, and it's all sorted out. But the day-to-day operations were seamless. English is so overrated.

Another major change that came not long after the move to the Buckhead building was that we started outsourcing deliveries. I struck a great deal with a local courier service and that part of the business started to run itself too.

Of course, I had one holdout from the "old days" of employee-delivered cakes. Drake still wanted to lend a hand. He enjoyed the residential Buckhead orders because he knew all those little streets. And, if something came up at the last minute, Drake was my guy. He'd show up for a couple of hours to deliver cakes. If he couldn't show up, it wasn't a big deal.

Everything ran much more smoothly, but we still had our quirks. Although there did seem to be more of a professional air about the company, nobody was ever going to mistake us for an insurance office or law firm.

Stinkyman Joe followed us from Howell Mill to Roswell Road. That's five miles. For a homeless person, I imagine that's like moving to another state. I was touched by his loyalty, to say the least. Well, I was 90 percent touched and 10 percent concerned about the new posh building and growing business coming complete with state-of-the-art mixers, a stunning storefront, a professional courier service, and our own homeless person.

One morning, he came by and asked about work, and I really didn't have anything. So, he asked to borrow our weed whacker to do some nearby lawns. I gave it to him.

Well, a couple hours later, I'm in the conference room entertaining three suits when he comes in. He stands right inside of the door, holds the weed whacker up in the air like he just yanked Excalibur from the stone, and cranks it up at full force.

The suits just about fell out of their chairs.

Meanwhile, I'm laughing, but you can't hear me (thank goodness) over the buzz of the weed whacker.

Then, Stinkyman Joe gives it a rest and says with a smile, "I just wanted to show you that it's still working, Miss Melissa."

# 23

## COOKIES, BITS, AND BYTES

At some point at Howell Mill, before we even made it to Buckhead, it's worth noting that a computer appeared in the office.

Since year one, my mother had been saying, "Melissa, you should put all your ingredients on the computer!" And I'd been retorting, "Mom, I can look across my living room floor and count four bags of flour!"

Well, it wasn't so easy counting all those bags of flour anymore, but that first computer made me nervous more than anything. We started using it to keep track of orders, but I still did them by hand, too, for backup.

Here, at 3215 Roswell Road, where we'd stay for the next seventeen years, computers would prove to be our game changer. And, Susannah, my new sidekick, would prove to be mine.

Because computers didn't blow up and the world didn't end after Y2K, I had to move forward, regardless of how leery I was about technology. So, Dan came back somewhere around 2002-ish to escort us into the twenty-first century.

Around this time, Susannah and I would start alternating being pregnant for the next seven years.

Susannah lived in Roswell (the city) and wanted to keep working, but the travel was too hard with a newborn. To solve this dilemma, we thought why not put these computers to the test and open a store for her right by her house, which was about twenty-five minutes away from our Roswell Road location in Buckhead.

Well, that was a smart idea! Susannah was rocking the satellite store, and she'd hired someone to work with her. At the end of every day, she'd fax orders in, and we'd add them to our already-in-existence baking grid on the computer. This worked for a stint. Then, Dan set it up so we could have multi-unit locations with all the orders going into the same place, like two people writing on Google Docs. My pre-Dan days had me buying into a software program from a baking convention that turned out to be a total flop. That was my single, biggest monetary mistake to date.

Dan would eventually come on board fulltime, and he's with us to this day.

## PEOPLE ARE, AND ALWAYS WILL BE, IMPORTANT

Although there's more sophistication to the way the company is run than I sometimes let on, Piece of Cake is not married to technology, by any means. We're still cracking eggs the old-fashioned way in the back of the house. The ordering system is indeed computerized, the mailing list is kept in a giant database, but the first cash register ever to make its way into the shop didn't arrive until the holiday season of 2002, when we entered our fifth year of netting seven figures annually.

It was like playing store. Everybody loved the new cash register. It was as if I'd given them a puppy for Christmas. Sweet, playful surprise!

# 24

## JAMES, JACK, AND LINDY

After settling into the new location on Roswell Road, embracing technology, and adjusting to the marked shift in staffing, I did this really cool thing: I got married and had two children.

When you're used to waking up at four or five in the morning to run a business five or six days a week for fifteen to twenty years and suddenly that stops, you think: *Hmm, what should I do with all this free time?* For me, it was start a family.

James and I traveled on the periphery of each other's social circles for probably decades. We were bound to meet eventually. And, when we did, back in 2003, it just felt right. We were married in 2004 at my mom's place in Buckhead. My childhood home was built on a magical piece of land. It was a beautiful garden wedding with hundreds of people in attendance.

Without further ado, on July 29, 2005, I gave birth to Jack Louis Jernigan. We didn't allot for a honeymoon period. There was less-than-zero time left to think about starting a family. But don't forget I started this company in my mid-twenties in the mid-eighties. James was on the same page, but he was also very reassuring that we weren't behind schedule. "You wouldn't have liked me all that much had we met a decade ago. Trust me, Melissa, the timing is perfect."

I wanted kids (plural). So, without delay, on November 19, 2007, my daughter, Lindy Bunnen Jernigan, arrived. James wanted four kids, but he would have needed to have successfully wooed me a decade back to make that happen. I was the one that reassured him this time that he could have the last two with his next wife if need be.

Jack, a summer baby, had Mom all to himself in the early days. But, Lindy was born a week before Thanksgiving. The first six weeks of her life were spent at POC.

Our engagement party invites
(James is a big Elvis fan)

# 25

## AND THEN THERE WERE EIGHT

We opened our next store in Decatur. It was a little bit harder to get there for deliveries, but one of our employees had a friend who wanted to run it, making it the next perfect storefront. *Bam.* Done. We'd deliver everything once a day in the mornings, and let people pick up their afternoon orders. This was how our distribution department was born. The Decatur store was a real dump, but the parking was sensational. People needed to park to grab their cakes, so that's what mattered to us. Now, customers were picking up their cakes exclusively at the Decatur location, which saved them money, too, on the delivery charge.

We invested in more satellite stores after that in Dunwoody, Vinings, and Camp Creek to name a few. But we were killing ourselves because we still weren't hiring on pace with the growth. *And by we, I mean me.* We were doing all the baking in Buckhead and distributing to a half dozen stores. (We would eventually add four more.) We had 3,500 square feet on Roswell Road, which helped because we'd tripled our space, but we had increased our sales by more than six-fold. At least before, we were able to expand from our original 800 square feet of basement. But in Buckhead? Damn, was my spatial reasoning off about the possibility of expanding there. At no point did I consider POC a corporate industry, and I was always dreaming big.

In an attempt to accommodate her expansion, I purchased an old semitrailer off a "retired" semitruck and ended up parking that in the back of the Roswell Road Store. This became our extra storage unit. It was neither convenient nor ideal, but for a stint (six years) we made do.

By the end, it was like being back in my condo.

For years, Robb kept saying, "Melissa, the fire department is going to bust in there and close up shop! You're way over capacity."

*Please, Robb, be serious. They love our cakes too much to do that....* (Besides, they were right next door.)

○ ○ ○

By 2016, we had fifty or more regular employees and were baking for eight satellite stores, including one at Hartsfield-Jackson Atlanta International Airport.

So, it's 2012, and there I am, sitting in the airport waiting on a plane, when this high school friend walks past me. "Steve, hi!" I shout, and then ask him where he's going, the universal "how are you?" when you run into someone in an airport.

Steve says, "Nowhere," and adds that he runs the commissaries at the airport.

"Oh..." I reply. "I'd love to have a Piece of Cake store here."

A year later, he calls and says, "Hi Melissa, it's Steve. I have a spot for you at the airport if you still want it."

The storefront there does not make the most money because of our contract with ATL, but it's worth it. We basically wholesale the product to them, so we're not technically running the store. But, oh, the marketing we get from that location. You can't put a price on that.

## SOMETIMES, YOU HAVE TO THINK INSIDE THE BOX: THE CAKE BOX!

# 26

## SHE'S BACK.

When Helen left, we'd kept in regular touch by phone, but we weren't able to see each other much. She was running around with three kids who were all heavily involved in sports, and POC was growing like a magic beanstalk for the first fifteen years of the twenty-first century.

At the mid-point, around 2007, I started to see Gamble and Mac around the store. That was a hoot. Mac, her youngest, born a year after she'd left, now in high school, had started on phones. We were gathering email addresses in addition to phone numbers by that point. People would say, "It's Bob underscore Smith at AOL dot com or it's Gloria underscore Washington at Hotmail dot com." And so on.... One day, Mac said (out loud unfortunately for him), "Who are all these Underscores? Sure is an odd name." After that, Mac was dubbed Underscore. It reminded me of the good ol' days. I didn't want to go back there, as that twenty-seven-year-old energy was but a dream, but I got a good chuckle.

A couple years after that, with Jack and Lindy in school fulltime, Helen and I started meeting in a neighborhood restaurant for lunch. She was doing marketing for the Children's Healthcare of Atlanta, sort of like my gig with Union Settlement back during my NYC stint.

"I'd been thinking we could use a solid marketing person," I casually said, just thinking out loud.

For two decades now I'd been the captain of the ship. But, by this time, I had a bakery manager, store operations manager, systems and technology department, and an HR person. And, while we marketed all the time and everyone knew the product, we did not have an official person in the position.

Months later, it was now 2011, we wound up on the same Home Tour of Atlanta. "Helen," I said, "you should come back to Piece of Cake when your commitment with the Children's Organization is over."

"Yeah, why not. Sounds great," she said.

Twenty-six years since we'd founded Piece of Cake, and twenty years after I'd bought her out of the company, Helen had returned. Just like that.

People would say, "Wow, she's back! What's her title?"

The title thing had never agreed with either one of us. We hadn't even settled on my title yet. *Back up, people, relax.*

But then I wondered, *What do we call Helen?* "How about Helen," I suggested to a few employees around the office one day. That idea was received with cold stares. "I guess Head of Marketing works if you can't roll with just Helen."

At that, they smiled. *Whatever.*

To this day, when I walk into my other stores, I say, "Hi, I'm Melissa." Some of my employees know me but some don't, as they might be new. If I'm with Helen, she'll generally add, "She owns the company. She's *that* Melissa." But without my spokeswoman there, I might come off like some extra friendly customer or a full-blown loon. Who knows? But I never add a title.

Despite the atmosphere being so different from when she'd left—*the bathrooms alone!*—we picked up where we'd left off.

People still ask if we had a falling out. I guess that'd make the story juicier, but we did not. People also ask, "If Helen were a man, do you think she would have returned as your employee?"

I don't know. Maybe, maybe not. We never had egos about anything. I couldn't tell you if that was a woman thing or an "us" trait.

Looking back, though, my present self would tell my past self "you can handle it" if I could. I had made such a big deal about her exodus, like the world was going to stop spinning. When you find someone you can trust, someone you really vibe with, it's rare and it's hard to let go.

But it became a wild and incredible ride, climbing the ladder of success with my POC family on my own. What an adventure.

I wouldn't change a thing.

And then, it was pure joy to have Helen return.

She loved the gift-shop-style storefront, and that we were selling slices. And, though neither one of us can recall how it all started, one day, we decided to take those slices on the road and start "caking some companies." This meant, that we'd just show up with free slices and surprise them. Marketing!

The idea was outstanding. But the thought of me having to walk into businesses, pitch POC, and leave cakes slices, free or not, sounded terrifying.

Helen was all over it.

We did this on Tuesdays for a couple of years until security tightened and we started getting kicked out of buildings. Keep in mind, these were Class A businesses. Security would track us down and accuse us of soliciting, which was a big no-no, and they'd boot us.

It was fun while it lasted. Next. Or so we thought.

But our cakes had left an impression.

Anyway, shortly after we stopped caking on Tuesdays, one of the companies contacted us. They missed us! They invited us to come back and cake them. Then, the domino effect occurred, and we started getting into more buildings.

o o o

Today, we "cake 'em" twice a week, on Tuesdays and Thursdays, going around Atlanta from business to business. In an hour's time, with two employees to pass out cake and collect the money, we sell four or five hundred individual slices. It's a real cardiovascular activity. But unlike spin class, it's one we love.

o o o

When we were getting ready to celebrate our thirtieth anniversary, we got together at the square conference table, all staring at each other, trying to figure out how we wanted to do this—market so all of Atlanta would know about the event. That's when I realized we market every day. I'm about as far from a salesperson as one could be, but you tell me to get it done and I can get it done. Same goes for my staff. We're always marketing. Therefore, the work is always complete, and the word is always out. I guess we did become Avon ladies after all, delivering our goods straight to your door.

### ALWAYS HAVE EVERYTHING DONE AHEAD OF TIME (IN CASE THE QUEEN INVITES YOU FOR TEA)

That's my mother's motto. Prepare in advance. I have always done this.

(Thank you, Mom.)

# 27

## TEN CAKE-ISMS FOR SUCCESS

I've always believed, like the great Yogi Berra, that if you come to a fork in the road, take it. This has gotten me through sad times, stressful times, and happy ones, too. And it's made my business what it is today.

∘ ∘ ∘

For the first ten years, all Piece of Cake did was sell cakes, and only a very specific list of cakes. I remember people calling in and asking for some particular type or flavor. "Well, it's not on our menu," we'd say, dragging out the "well" with a sweet Southern drawl, hoping to keep the customer calm.

"Can I special order?"

"*Welllll*, no, we don't do special orders, but you ought to try our Strawberry Cake. It's our top seller this week." If it was in the fall, we'd push Pumpkin Cake, in the spring, we'd talk up our Lemon Cake, and so on. We stayed true to the business and did not deviate.

In the first two years, we grew the company on just three products: Chocolate Layer Cake with fudge frosting, Carrot Cake with Cream Cheese Frosting, and Sour Cream Coffee Cake. In year three, though we offered a cake of the month by then, we rolled in a few more regulars, two of which were Red Velvet Cake and, thanks to my mother's love of dingoes, our thirty-years-and-counting-best-seller, White Chocolate Layer Cake. We were focused on what we were doing and didn't spread ourselves too thin doing other things. We weren't jacks-of-all-trades, but masters of one great thing.

## BE CONCRETE WITH YOUR IDEA AND STAY IN YOUR LANE

It wasn't just that it looked like Helen and I had (each) drank a bottle of Boons Farm before writing *"Happy Birthday, George"* on a cake that made us say, "Just say no to writing on cakes!" *What if somebody changes their mind? Then we're stuck with this George cake. How are we going to sell that?* It was a lot more economical to add a tiny note card. Which people love, by the way—the tinier the better!

(ACTUAL SIZE of our note cards today)

We got a lot of inquiries for wedding cakes. Even though I didn't mention it earlier, we dabbled in theme-based cakes in the beginning. It was a short-lived dabble, more of a dibble, as we didn't have the time, patience, or talent for that sort of thing any more than we did for scribbling on cakes. Not to mention the cakes weighed a lot already. They didn't need to be bogged down with stick figurines playing sports or horsies or Disney characters. As for wedding cakes? The stress of weddings on brides-to-be had us steering clear of that carnival from the onset.

We were here to have fun (damnit!).

## MAKE SURE THE HASSLE IS WORTH THE REWARD

As Helen was exiting the company back in '91, shipping was entering it. A pound cake is to the world of cakes what vanilla is to ice cream. It's basic and reliable and everybody likes it. This was the first cake we figured out how to ship, which expanded our market considerably. My college friends were our pound cake guinea pigs for the first few shipping experiments. They were thrilled to get packages and report back if it made it there "alive and edible."

Our initial wrapping efforts were so problematic. We'd watched Helen's sister, Margaret, use this blow-dryer method in the gift shop, so we tried to do it that way, but it's a delicate process. We'd burn a hole in the plastic and have to redo it every time, but we stuck with this homespun and ineffective process for a couple years until we invested in a shrink wrap machine. This goes back to me not wanting to invest company money until I knew our adventure in shipping would be a lasting success. But it also plays into my innate tenacity. When I get my mind focused on something, there's little that can stop me, least of all "reason." I had a feeling that shipping cakes would be worth the effort.

Once, when the shrink wrap machine was on the blink, we had to borrow one from the Big Star grocery store across the street. It was the holidays, and we were slammed. A week later, when I was out on a special delivery, the meat guy came and said he needed it back. On returning to the office and learning that he'd taken it, I marched into Big Star and said, "I'm sorry, but I'm not giving that up yet. Y'all have more than one. I see two right there!" The meat guy, of course, handed it over.

And then there I was, this crazy person wheeling a giant shrink wrap machine across a busy street midday. I knew at that point I was a woman not to be messed with.

We ship cakes to all fifty states today, comprising 15 to 20 percent of our annual revenue. It is not cheap, but....

Cary, our bakery manager, used to work for a national bakery before signing on at POC. Normally, new employees watched how the vets were doing it, did their best to catch on, and hit the bricks if they couldn't keep up. Not in his case— talk about efficiency. Rolling a bakery manager into the company has been free of hassle and replete with rewards.

## FEMALE INTUITION IS THE REAL MOTHER OF INVENTION

We've always believed the customer is always right.

*Or have we?*

One of our regulars, an artist, would frequently call to complain that his cake had melted. Standard procedure at Piece of Cake was to replace a cake if anyone had an issue. But, after a string of replacements for "Picasso," Page said he was going over there to investigate the cake melting mishaps himself. On that, he grabbed his badge, DNA kit, his replacement cake, and took off. It was a scorching summer day in July.

Page came back an hour later with the replacement cake in hand, having solved the mystery. "It was, like, 300 degrees in there," he said. "The man does not believe in air conditioning. I told him that was enough monkey business and no more free cakes."

If a customer was a particularly bad troublemaker, the staff might go so far as to fire them.

There was this one woman who was a natural-born scammer. Combine that with her full figure and penchant for cake, and we had a situation.

She'd cut herself a big old piece, quartering a cake that was meant to be divided into twelve or more slices. This was her angle. Then, after having eaten 25 percent of the product, she'd call stating it just wasn't up to standard.

*"This cake tastes different than the last one."*

*"Did you change your fudge frosting recipe?"*

*"I said easy on the sprinkles."*

*"Is that...a plastic bug?!"*

Then, she'd demand to have the cake replaced. One day, she brought the cake back in herself. Well, Natalie had had it. She opened the cake box and there sat a perfectly beautiful White Chocolate Layer Cake with a big piece cut out.

Natalie looked her straight in the eye and said, "That cake's fine. You're not getting another one. And, ma'am, you can't be our customer anymore."

And that was the day we realized we could fire the really bad customers.

We took it to the computer, which we were savvy with by that point, and created a list of the customers we were blackballing, making it official. What fun!

Page fired a few customers himself. One was a woman who'd always dressed well, heels and all. She lived on one of the nicest streets in town. Nonetheless, he caught her stealing individually wrapped slices of cake, squirreling them, like money from a vault, into her Gucci Supreme Tote. "Ma'am, I am sorry, but you cannot be our customer anymore. Good day."

None of us relished dealing with unhappy customers, though, so, in true Piece of Cake fashion, we all pitched in and took turns handling the ornery ones. Somebody would call and say, "Can I please speak to the owner?" in that angry uptight voice, you know the one I'm talking about, the one that's 2.5 seconds away from irate. And I'd go, "Who wants to be the owner today?" And Harriet or Natalie or Fuzz or Weazer 2 would volunteer.

It was a beautiful thing. And onto Blackballed.doc they went.

## BEING CUSTOMER-CENTRIC DOES NOT MEAN BEING A DOORMAT

We opened a shop in Charlotte, North Carolina, after my college friend, Angela, suggested we do so. (No, she wasn't in marketing. I think she just liked the cakes.) There were a couple of girls up there that wanted to run it. One of them had worked for POC before relocating. They had a cute little store in mind, and the girls were ready to go. We went back and forth on how it was going to work out, deciding I'd own it and they'd run it. They would fax their orders into us in Atlanta, and we would ship them off. In theory, it was a good idea. But, to launch anything, even a remote branch of a successful business, required mounds of dedication. We learned this the hard way, of course (and over the course of three years). I'd been driving there like a mad woman and we'd been shipping orders too.

Then one day, around three in the afternoon, I called. No one answered. Hmm? I did this a few more times. They'd gone home for the day. At three. My vision for the Charlotte branch was not a boutique shop that didn't pull in serious numbers. What was the point? It became such a pain in the neck. They were like my kids, these girls, but, well, I let 'em go (so maybe they were more like step-kids.) Plus, my heart was in Atlanta more than Charlotte and I didn't want to spend my life driving back and forth for one shop.

## SOMETIMES, GOING WITH THE FLOW MEANS LETTING GO

Despite my apprehensions about trusting computers, times had changed with the Age of Technology upon us. The only way to evolve was to be forward thinking about the business. This was not my area of expertise, and it didn't feel like there was a recipe I could look up and follow. Dan was the man to teach me how to grow the company in a cost-effective manner. (Well, not so much teach me as do it for me.) I recognized early on the importance of surrounding myself with intelligent people with different skillsets. I've never thought I was the smartest person in the room, but I'm headstrong in my ideas. That's my strength.

The key to expansion for a company like Piece of Cake was to apply technology without adding back-end costs (excessive staffing and operating space and equipment). We became high tech in the front office and remained low tech in the kitchen. If you want to grow ten stores but you have to add ten times the number of people, this is neither cost-effective nor efficient. You'd be producing more product, but not necessarily increasing the value of the company or its bank account. You want to add ten stores and ten times the product, but with as little overhead as possible. Dan's skillset is to build processes and integrate technology. Everyone needs a Dan if they want to expand their company, is my point.

## SURROUND YOURSELF WITH TALENT UNLIKE YOUR OWN

In 2019, we opened two more stores in SunTrust and Brookwood, and the only people we needed to pay were in the storefront serving the customers. You can't get away from that if you're a full-service business—if customers are dining in or if you have to bake the product on the premises. If you have to hire back-end function in every store, that gets expensive with salaries and insurance, etc. But if you only need one or two people manning the store and taking the orders, then you can get the work done back at the mother ship. Even for deliveries, you just need one person to sign at drop-off in the mornings. With everything computerized, a couple of people can do what six, eight, or ten did twenty years ago. The operation is such that we can have a light day and bake 400 cakes or a heavy one and bake 900, and the same staff can handle the variance in volume. Keep in mind, we are still a labor-intensive operation. Part of the efficiency comes from communication between stores. And the generous size of the kitchen allows for the swing in volume.

We have ten locations now, but it's mostly a matter of which trucks to stock with which product in the morning, and our programming system directs us to each store, taking the work out of it. (This is a simplified way of explaining it.)

Today, during the holidays, we still hire temps, but they don't need to be highly trained or knowledgeable, as they follow cues from the system. Computers can't replace my Cakers, and I wouldn't even want them to. But if you want to grow your business, technology can serve you well.

We still run the kitchen the old-fashioned way, cracking eggs and beating batter. The front of the office is what's so technology driven. But there are always things in my industry that will never be replaced by a computer, which is one of the reasons I built a business like this. For the first twenty years, this was my community. It was about the people and for the people in my Atlantan Universe. Now, I'm married and have my own community of people at home, so technology serves me well these days.

## DON'T JUST BE OPEN TO CHANGE, IMPLEMENT IT

Piece of Cake started leasing out space to a growing number of complementary businesses back in the late nineties. The "Bread Girl," as she's always been called by the Cakers, was one of our first long-time tenants, renting a tiny footprint of space to market her fresh-baked breads. We had a "Casserole Girl," selling pre-cooked dishes that customers could grab on their way home for dinner. Women-owned businesses have always gravitated to us and we've made room. There have been soy candles, homemade lollipops, etc., so many unique complementary items. These may seem odd adjuncts to the business but, actually, they're right in line with the essence of Piece of Cake, which has more to do with being a community hub than with baked goods. You can't exactly gauge the benefits of these symbiotic relationships, but they all matter. They all make a difference, and it feels good.

## CONNECTION EQUALS SUCCESS

People have never stopped wanting me to take on a partner.

I've been victim to more pitches than I can count over the years, and all the candidates were men. Even my female friends have asked (still ask) if I'd partner with a man "this time."

I considered one businessperson, one time, "Mr. X," and it wasn't because of his male status.

It was around 2004. Mr. X came in at the right time with a deal that felt about 75 percent right. I wanted to get to the next level and wasn't sure how.

Mr. X had a proposal on how to make POC go national, get her into some major retail outlets. I was excited about the possibilities. I didn't have my kids yet, which meant my mind had all this free space to devote to POC's growth.

But in the end, it didn't fly.

The turning point in our relationship came one day when we were sitting in my office. Lord knows what we were chatting about, as I'm the queen of getting off track. One second, we'd be all nuts, bolts, and numbers, in a POC quarterly meeting, the next minute we'd be planning someone's thirtieth birthday bash.

Anyway....

Mr. X was always trying to yank my chain a little bit, and my chain is not easily yanked. But, on this particular day, he was explaining why he was worth more than me, validating the proposed salary he was negotiating. Of course, I never think I'm worth anything but that's my own issue. Did Mr. X have all this experience? Yes. On a certain level, he was right about the value he could bring to the company. I was even beginning to slant in his direction. Then, he added that he had a family to support and I had no one. Therefore, he should make more money.

I blew a gasket.

At which point, he started laughing.

"Is this funny to you? So, if I had children at home, I'd be worth more to this company? Is that what you're saying?"

"No, if you had children at home, you might be worth less, as you'd have to take time off to, you know, watch them."

At that, I blew a dozen gaskets.

"Melissa, calm down," Mr. X pleaded. "All I'm saying is, I have to go to work every—"

"I have to go to work every day!"

"But I'm the head of the household—"

"I'm the head of the household!"

Mr. X had never seen me mad before, and we'd been negotiating this partnership for about a year.

"I'm just saying that you're a wom—"

"I can't believe you're going there. I'm a woman? So, I'm worth less than you, even in my own company. You chauvinistic son of a BEEP!"

"Someone's getting feisty. How about we calm down and talk about this like men."

"Oh, Lord, you've done it now!"

"I didn't mean "men" men, Melissa. You know what I meant. It's a phrase!"

Oh, I knew what he meant. I booted Mr. X from my office with a speech that had some derivation of the word chauvinist in it half a dozen more times.

And that was that.

I was disappointed that it didn't work out, but also relieved. It would have meant working so much harder. But it would have been an exciting ride. It would have been what

I've always wanted: to expand POC into the ocean, so she can stretch her fins alongside the great whites.

o o o

A note about the pandemic: We had to shut down for five to six weeks, as so many other businesses did. (And I thought cake was essential???) I was afraid for my employees more than anything. The future seemed so unpredictable. Fortunately, we reopened before long, but we weren't impervious to the new climate with which we had to navigate. Some stores were hit harder than others by the loss in business, and we had to pivot—the buzzword of the year—to keep the company going.

We seem to be on track again a year later, focusing on keeping the business streamlined until the world finds its new normal. My heart goes out to the businesses that have not survived this unprecedented time in history and to those still struggling.

# FINAL THOUGHTS

When I was two months old, my grandmother Ruth Alice Norman Weil Halsband had a massive stroke at the age of sixty. She became paralyzed on her whole right side. My mom left me, her newborn, to go be with her mother in Europe. The circumstances were dire, and she had to go where she was needed most.

My grandmother was a very international woman, and the fact that she'd been born in the early part of the twentieth century didn't stop her. Well, it inhibited her from doing some things. She wanted to go to med school, but it was the 1940s. New York University didn't allow women to become doctors. So, she obtained a PhD in Organic Chemistry, instead. Then, she built a lab on her family's farm in Westchester County in Upstate New York and made a name for herself as a scientist.

Talk about an outlier.

After the stroke, my grandmother had to learn to do everything with her left hand, from personal hygiene to writing, painting, cooking, chemistry, needlepoint, you name it. My mother nursed her through the first two crucial months. Then, she came back to me, and, in her magical Lucinda way, she reattached the umbilical cord and we've been living symbiotically ever since.

I believe my drive is genetic and generations deep, but also living by example for your children makes an impression. We learn by example.

Growing up, I was well connected to a lot of shining examples of hardworking adults. And I have always had great friends. And I did date during the mayhem, even though I didn't bring it up much. Somehow, I knew I wouldn't settle down until my dream was ready to be on her own, like when you say you'll do something for yourself—take salsa lessons, go to Europe, join a book club—as soon as the kids go off to college. I planned to marry and have kids when POC went off to college. And, as you know, I did.

I recently went to the closing for one of my mom's photo exhibits that was hanging at a gallery in Midtown. One of the attendees asked her where she found the inspiration to create the body of work that was showcased. They were select photos from over the course of her career.

She said, "I stumbled upon them. Everything just happened serendipitously. When you come to a fork in the road, take it. I went with it."

Somewhere in the middle of this sea of art enthusiasts, I was swallowing the lump in my throat and blinking back tears. *I thought that was my motto.*

I was talking to someone the other day about projecting, and I was thinking if you live right and keep doing the right thing, you don't have to cover your bases. I've always tried to do that, never wavering.

Robb has said of my journey and my success that if you toss me a ball, I'll flail about like I'm drunk, blind, and crazy, but catch it every time. "Melissa's the luckiest person in the history of America." He's attested to that, chuckling, at many a family gathering.

I don't know if I can claim number one status, but I do feel fortunate.

I still get those sideways glances, but they're glazed in curiosity instead of skepticism these days.

What can I say? I come from a long line of outliers.

o o o

I started Piece of Cake because I didn't want to be a slave to the nine-to-five. I wanted my life's work to be fun and original. I wanted it to be bigger than me and to do something that mattered. (Yes, I realize baking cakes is not brain surgery.) Even back in college I aspired to that, even though I thought my destiny was pointing me toward nonprofit. POC just happened to suit my personality better. I've always been about people. As soon as we started the company, I thought: *This feels right.*

Piece of Cake began with a product that satisfied your sweet tooth, but it's really not about that anymore.

It's a place that provides jobs. It's a good place to be. It offers flexibility, so if you need to take a vacation, you take a vacation. When someone screws up a batch of cakes, it's not like the end of the world. I'm not down people's throats. It's just not all about the business to me. It's about connection. It's a community that doesn't just provide a product, we're involved locally with charities and other nonprofits.

When I talk about POC with my past and present employees or hear them reminisce, they don't talk about the cakes, either. I hear them giggle about how they used to work to the point of delirium and then go out for drinks afterward. I hear about the times they've helped each other out of scrapes, and how they teased each other mercilessly. I hear about connections made—including several marriages—and friendships forged, about years and years of inside jokes, and about how everyone they knew with more conventional jobs wanted to hang out at Piece of Cake along with them.

Piece of Cake is, perhaps, not the center of the entire universe, but it's a wonderful world created from love of community.

A hundred years ago back in my condo kitchen (*trust me, it feels that long ago*), I envisioned growing carrots and blueberries for the cakes. (God knows where. Maybe on my sunporch next to the two ovens from Goodwill.) And I kept telling Helen that I wanted to get a big basket on my bike, so I could combine my favorite pastime with work. *Can you picture me at your doorstep, out of breath, drenched in sweat, a tower of cake boxes balancing precariously in a basket on the front of my ten-speed?*

Things sure did turn out differently.

My friends say I'm like a duck floating on a placid lake, all calm and content on the outside, with feet fluttering like mad underneath the surface of the water.

After all these years, I still don't have a plan. But I do know we can't stay the same. If you're not moving forward, you're moving backward. And I've never seen a duck paddle backward before, have you?

I don't know what the future looks like for Piece of Cake, but I'm always working toward being ready for it. I'm on the lookout in a very subtle way.

We used to never even sell slices, and then it took on a life of its own. You're defined by "baking and delivering cakes" but not limited by it because...you never know.

I'm not about tooting my own horn, God help me. I thrive from behind the scenes. But I do have some tidbits and I wanted to share.

Even with the writing of this book, which started ten years ago and then stopped, I've relied on instinct. The time wasn't right. And then, last year, some new people came into my life, and the time was right. Most of my forward motion is based on a feeling, a pull, or a direct order from POC herself.

We're not quite a bakery and we've never fit into a category. We're more like a cakery, but not exactly. Just like this book, we can't be pigeon-holed.

*What is this book, anyway?*

It's a memoir, a business book, a book about baked goods that's not about baking. It's a comedy, a comedy of errors, a story about family and friendship.

This book is about a journey. A hero's journey? If we're all heroes, then, sure. This is a book about my heroes. It's about listening to your mother, to the voices in your head (just some of them!), and to the universe. It's a book about madness and mayhem, hard work and happiness, surrender and synergy.

This is a book about doing it my way. Thanks for being a part of it but stay tuned.

Because this is just the end of the beginning....

# THE CAKE-ISMS

1. A BAD FIRST JOB CAN BE A GREAT BEGINNING
2. IF IT STOPS BEING FUN, GET OUT!
3. TIMING REALLY IS EVERYTHING
4. FEEL THE FEAR AND BAKE IT ANYWAY
5. SOMETIMES, THE MOST OBVIOUS SOLUTION IS *THE MOST OBVIOUS SOLUTION*
6. LISTEN TO YOUR MOTHER (MOST OF THE TIME)
7. GROW WITH THE FLOW
8. EVERY DAY IS BLACK FRIDAY AT PIECE OF CAKE
9. NEVER UNDERESTIMATE THE POWER OF A COMPLIMENT
10. IF YOU'RE WORKING WITH A PREGNANT PERSON...THEY WILL EVENTUALLY GIVE BIRTH
11. IF CHANGE FINDS YOU, LEAP INTO HER ARMS
12. DON'T LEAVE BABIES OR BAGS OF MONEY UNATTENDED
13. AUTONOMY IS ITS OWN REWARD
14. DO NOT UNDERESTIMATE THE POWER OF ORGANIZED CHAOS
15. PEOPLE ARE, AND ALWAYS WILL BE, IMPORTANT
16. SOMETIMES YOU HAVE TO THINK INSIDE THE BOX: THE CAKE BOX!
17. ALWAYS HAVE EVERYTHING DONE AHEAD OF TIME (IN CASE THE QUEEN INVITES YOU FOR TEA)
18. BE CONCRETE WITH YOUR IDEA AND STAY IN YOUR LANE
19. MAKE SURE THE HASSLE IS WORTH THE REWARD
20. FEMALE INTUITION IS THE REAL MOTHER OF INVENTION
21. BEING CUSTOMER-CENTRIC DOES NOT MEAN BEING A DOORMAT
22. SOMETIMES, GOING WITH THE FLOW MEANS LETTING GO
23. SURROUND YOURSELF WITH TALENT UNLIKE YOUR OWN
24. DON'T JUST BE OPEN TO CHANGE, IMPLEMENT IT
25. CONNECTION EQUALS SUCCESS

## A Note to the Reader

There are so, so many people that have helped me along the way, and I cannot thank everyone. If your name was not mentioned in these pages, you are no less appreciated. I did not do this alone. Please know that you brought something special to the table and I am, and always will be, so appreciative. I cannot reiterate this enough. I am grateful every day for the blessings this career brings into my life.

And thank you so much for reading about my journey from banking to baking. I hope you enjoyed it. If you feel so inspired, leave a review on Amazon.

—Melissa Bunnen Jernigan

# End Notes

Introduction
His pizza has become the standard by which all other pizzas in Japan are judged to this day.
https://www.pmq.com/made-in-japan-the-secrets-of-tokyo-neapolitan-style-pizza/

Chapter 1, page 4
In a jiffy (how I did most things), I found employment with Union Settlement in Harlem, a nonprofit that provided education, wellness, and community-building programs.
https://unionsettlement.org/

Chapter 5, page 23
People were making money and spending it, and big business was back with a vengeance, which was ultimately our target market.
https://www.thoughtco.com/us-economy-in-the-1980s-1148148

Chapter 20, page 105
Today, one in five firms with over one million dollars in annual revenue is owned by a woman.
www.nawbo.org/resources/women-business-owner-statistics

Piece of Cake